FOUNDATION
OF THE CHARLOTTE
JEWISH COMMUNITY

Donated by

Rabbi and Mrs. Harold I. Krantzler

in honor of their 10 years

at Temple Beth-El

July 20, 1986

Speizman Jewish Library
at Shalom Park
5007 Providence Road
Charlotte, NC 28211

HERZL AS I REMEMBER HIM

ERWIN ROSENBERGER

HERZL
AS I REMEMBER HIM

*Translated from the German
and abridged by*
Louis Jay Herman

HERZL PRESS • NEW YORK • 1959

PRINTED IN THE UNITED STATES OF AMERICA BY
MARSTIN PRESS, INC., NEW YORK CITY
I. LONDON, *President*

Dedicated
to my dear wife ERNESTINE

ILLUSTRATIONS

Editor's Note

We wish to acknowledge our indebtedness to Dr. ALEX
BEIN, Director of the Zionist Central Archives, Jerusalem,
who first called our attention to the manuscript of this book.
Thereupon we contacted DR. ERWIN ROSENBERGER in Florence, Italy, where he has been living for the last few years,
and obtained from him the original German manuscript.

I

BEFORE ME LIE DIARIES in which years ago I recorded my experiences and observations. Stacked next to them are various papers, correspondence, publications, manuscripts which have already passed through the printer's hands, and other documents.

Many of the pages are already yellowing. Half a century has passed over them. Fifty years. And over some of them even a few years more.

And yet—the persons and events still stand as vividly before my inner eye as though I had taken leave of them only yesterday....

It was on February 8, 1896 that I first saw the man who was to influence so greatly the course of my life. That evening, Dr. Theodor Herzl appeared as guest at a lecture in the clubroom of the *Jüdische Akademiche Lesehalle,* the Jewish students' society, in Vienna's 9th District.

Previously, Herzl had never appeared, publicly or semipublicly, in Viennese Jewish student circles or at other city meeting-places. This day was a memorably one for him; it was memorable and heavy with consequences for us students, too—indeed, for all Jewry, when one considers the important role played in the Zionist movement by the Jewish students of Vienna.

What had drawn us, a hundred or so university students, to the modest rooms of our club was a talk by the Chief Rabbi of Vienna, Dr. Moritz Güdemann.

I must confess that the name "Theodor Herzl" had meant little to me until then. My fellow students occasionally mentioned the writer Theodor Herzl in conversation, but I had yet to read anything he had written.

We had heard a rumor that Herzl planned to join our ranks, to fight with us for the Jewish and Zionist cause. When he now made his appearance—his début, so to speak —in the Jewish students' society, he was greeted with enthusiastic applause.

How unfamiliar the name "Theodor Herzl" was to me then is evident from the diary entry in which I recorded his presence at the club: I incorrectly spelled his name "Herzel" throughout. Yet, even then, when I saw him for the first time, his personality and what he said seem to have made a particular impression on me; for I sat down that very evening, at a late hour, to preserve what had happened for all time in the pages of my diary.

While Chief Rabbi Güdemann delivered his lecture, several guests, including Herzl, sat to the right of the small speaker's platform, facing the audience of students. Thus, I was able to glance at Herzl from time to time.

There were no women in the audience. In those days, women university students were a rarity, and our society had no female members.

Chief Rabbi Güdemann, a personable man of medium height in his early sixties, with a white patriarchal beard, had chosen "The Mission of the Jews" as the subject of his lecture. For the most part, however, he dealt with a particular theme: In contrast to other religious communities, the Jews have no missionaries. It is not customary among the Jews to send out special proselytizers to convert members of other religions to the Jewish faith.

Listening to these familiar things with only half an ear, I let my attention wander from time to time to the hitherto unknown Dr. Theodor Herzl. What a striking appearance! The prototype of the handsome Oriental. The cut of his features, the dark hair, the dark beard and moustache, the dark eyes all proclaimed eloquently that here sat a son of the East—and one of the noblest blood.

I found myself almost wondering: How does *he* come to be sitting on that plain chair? He would look perfectly at ease on the throne of a Babylonian king. How does that slim figure come to be wearing a modern business suit—that figure which was so obviously created for the robes on an Oriental prince? I was convinced that, if we had called a passerby into the room and said to him, "Here among the hundred of us there is a king in disguise; find him," the stranger would unhesitatingly have pointed to Herzl.

Thus my thoughts ran on. In the meantime, Dr. Güdemann finished his lecture, and it seemed as though the students had been merely waiting for it to end in order to turn impatiently to the truly interesting part of the evening. In an instant, Herzl was surrounded by members of our club and of other Jewish student societies and was caught up in a lively conversation.

I took no notice of the departure of the Chief Rabbi and several of the older guests of honor, although they included the architect Fleischer and the publisher of the Jewish *Österreichische Wochenschrift*, Dr. Josef B. Bloch.

The students crowded about Herzl, we younger ones yielding the places nearest him to our older comrades.

He began to speak at once in the middle of the room rather than on the podium; it was like a friendly private conversation and yet like a kind of official platform speech. Standing nearest him were little Dr. Jacob Kohn, Isidor Schalit of the Jewish academic society "Kadimah," Sofer of the "Ivria," Carl Pollak and Martin Engländer of the "Unitas," and Markus Ernst, one of the founders of the academic club "Gamala." All but Dr. Kohn were medical students.

We were equally captivated by Herzl's personality, by what he said and by how he said it. He stood in a relaxed attitude, his head bent slightly forward, his expressive dark eyes fixed now on one of us, now on another.

Herzl told us that his pamphlet, *The Jewish State*, would appear shortly.

"A regular state?" he was asked, "a real state on its own territory, with its own laws, inhabited, governed and administered by Jews?"

"Yes," Herzl said. "Our Jewish state will be just such a state. An independent state like Austria, France and England. Jews from all countries will found it and settle it. . . ."

His eyes searched our faces. These young people—would they smile in disbelief or amusement, would they raise objections?

Nothing of the sort happened. There were, to be sure, skeptical and irreverent souls among us, but this man, who spoke so matter-of-factly of a Jewish state, inspired a deep trust in us. . . . A Jewish state, an actual state—yes, it was undeniably a daring, sensational idea which at first might well leave the listener dumbfounded. Yet, it was really no more than the logically and courageously thought-through conclusion of the idea which we Jewish societies had always championed, albeit in a relatively rudimentary form: The Jewish people refuses to perish; it wants to live, to live—and if possible on its own soil. . . .

"And where will you find the Moses who will lead the Jews there?" cried a voice from the rear, over the heads of those in front. It was not the voice of one of us students. The question had been asked by Rabbi Löwy, a man in his seventies with a gentle smile, who often attended our affairs as a guest.

Courteously, Herzl went over to the old gentleman. They introduced themselves, and the ranks closed around them. "A Moses?" asked Herzl. "If he is not to be found, we will create him."

Dr. Jacob Kohn, obviously aroused by the reference to Moses, interjected: "Moses led the Jews about in the desert for forty years before he could bring them into the Promised Land."

"With modern transportation facilities, it will take forty hours," replied Herzl.

Dr. Kohn had not actually meant to raise an objection; rather, he meant: Let's think this matter over carefully. . . .

At any rate, these were no weighty counter-arguments. Herzl gently brushed them aside and told us:

"I myself assembled all the arguments which could possibly be cited against my pamphlet and then refuted them one after the other. Then I went and read it to the Chief Rabbi of Paris, Zadok Kahn. He sent for four leading French Jews, and I told them what I proposed in the pamphlet. They voiced their misgivings about this point or that. But it was a simple matter to reply to them. For I merely heard the same objections which I had thought of myself, and I had only to say, 'The answer to your question is on page 25 of the pamphlet, on page 28, 34, namely...,' and I cited the passages."

It was a pleasure to listen to Herzl, to look into his bold, yet kindly and intelligent eyes. There was no fanaticism in his melodious voice—only vigorous conviction and the calm assurance of a man who knows what he wants and what he is saying.

Herzl went on: "A territory for the Jewish state? We will ask the Sultan of Turkey to give us Palestine; in return, we will put his finances in order. The Jews will undoubtedly be able to provide the money and also the necessary *sechel.*"

Rabbi Löwy broke in once again. "We need the month of *Kislev,*" he said mysteriously.

"The month of *Kislev?*" Herzl did not understand, nor did the rest of us.

"*Kis* means 'pocket' in Hebrew; *lev* is 'heart,'" explained the old man.

Herzl acknowledged the pun with a smile and took up the thread of his discourse once again: "In my pamphlet, I suggest Argentina in addition to Palestine as a state territory. Why? We are among ouselves here, and I can tell you the reason: It's so the people in Constantinople won't think that we have our hearts set exclusively on a piece of Turkish territory and that they can name any price they want for it."

To a question dealing with the problem of agriculture, Herzl replied: "We will prapare the land with the most modern methods; we will work with the newest British and American machinery."

When he said, "We need the youth!" old Rabbi Löwy

sighed and remarked in a tone of resignation: "Then I will have to stay here."

"That isn't so," Herzl comforted him. "The young people are the advance guard, the pioneers, but there will be enough room for the older ones who come later."

An eager student asked timidly what Herzl meant by the term "infiltration," which he had used a little while before.

"By 'infiltration,'" Herzl explained, "I mean the slow, sporadic settlement of foreign territory ... here a few dozen Jews, there a few hundred ... on Turkish soil in Palestine, in Argentina, in Baron Hirsch's Jewish colonies. . . . In that way, we'll only bring anti-Semitism to Argentina. . . . I said as much to Baron Hirsch. . . . That means expecting the people there to live in mud huts. We don't need that; we'll build ourselves houses up to the sky. . . ."

He raised his arm slightly to indicate the houses going up.

"We will do it differently," he said, "first the land, then the colonization. First we must be the legal owners of a whole territory; afterward we can make it arable and build it up, not in bits and snatches, but on a grand scale."

Dr. Kohn remarked that he knew an engineer, a first-rate expert in the field of railroad construction and colonization, in the event Herzl would like to meet him.

"We would have to have a party organ, a newspaper," said Markus earnestly.

"That will come of itself," replied Herzl. "It will sprout out of the ground, and suddenly it will just be there."

It was remarkable how rapidly a *rapport* was estab-lished between Herzl and the students. And how swiftly and automatically, from the very first moment, his au-thority asserted itself and was acknowledged by us.

No one had ever appeared among us before this whom we wished to follow as eagerly as we did this Dr. Theodor Herzl. "We need the youth!" he had said earlier, and the wish, no sooner uttered, than it was fulfilled. We were all ready to serve him and his idea; he now had the youth which he wanted.

We heard many other things from Herzl's lips, that evening in the students' society, which won us over to his ideas and to the man himself. I will return to that later.... Suddenly, almost in the midst of making a point, Herzl broke off and looked at his watch. "I must conclude now," he said like someone who was nearly late for an appointment. "I have to leave."

Carl Pollak at once sent one of the first-year students to hail a carriage, and a two-horse rig promptly drove up. After directing a few final words of admonition to us in the entrance hall, Herzl took his leave with a comradely handshake; and, accompanied by our assurances of sup-port, he left—our Herzl.

2

A FEW DAYS LATER, I SAW HERZL at the *Maximilianplatz*. By his side was an elderly gentleman. They were walking slowly, absorbed in their thoughts. It seemed to me that there was a resemblance in their features. (Later, I learned that Herzl's companion of that day had been his father.)

Even if Herzl had been alone, I would scarcely have had the courage—indeed, the audacity—to address him in the street and tell him what a lasting impression his words had made. Hence, I contented myself with a silent but noticeable gesture of greeting, raising my hat almost as though in homage. He, too, raised his hat with a friendly smile, and I had the impression that he was pleasantly surprised at being thus greeted in the street by a completely unknown young man—perhaps a Jewish student who was drawn by his idea of a Jewish state.

A well-dressed young woman walking in front of me turned her head ever so slightly as Herzl passed. Perhaps she knew who he was. And, then again, perhaps she had simply been struck by the sight of this man with the majestic black beard.

One of those present in the students' society when Herzl made his "début" was my friend Markus Ernst, a medical student in a higher class than mine. As we left late that evening, he had expressed his astonishment that the name Theodor Herzl was so unfamiliar to me. "The man is a star of the first magnitude in the Viennese literary and journalistic world," he told me. "What's more, he is a member of the editorial staff of the *Neue Freie Presse*. His brilliant *feuilletons* in the *Presse* have won him the name of 'the *feuilleton* king' here in Vienna. He has also written books. Until recently, he was Paris correspondent for his paper. He is a prominent figure in Vienna society."

I tried to explain my ignorance: "I have so much to do these days—you'll have to make allowances for these gaps in my knowledge." I added: "Then we should be honored that this man favored our club with a visit?"

"We certainly should," Ernst replied emphatically.

It had seemed curious to me that anti-Semitism had gone completely unmentioned that historic evening at the club. The reason was not that anti-Semitism was regarded as a trifle; rather, its existence was so generally known, it was taken so much for granted, that there was no need to waste words over it. At that very time, the Imperial capital of Vienna was the scene of crude manifestations of anti-Semitism. On Saturday evening, February 8, while Herzl was speaking to us at the club, feverish preparations for the Vienna Municipal Council elections of February 27 were under way in all the clubhouses of the anti-Semitic Christian Social party. With acute eruptions of a centuries-old evil occurring in the city, Herzl preferred to ignore the "issues of the day" and speak instead of the Jewish state, which we hoped would one day carry us beyond the reach of anti-Semitism.

"We will have a flag, too," Herzl told us that evening. "Our banner is white and has seven stars.... That represents the seven-hour work day." He gazed over our heads for an instant, as though he could already see the flag waving.

"It is very important," he continued, "that the pamphlet in which I propose the Jewish state should be discussed as much as possible. I am willing to engage in discussion, but"—he added threateningly—"anyone who opposes me in a cheap way will have a hard time of it; I will make him look utterly ridiculous."

Markus Ernst asked what form of government the state would have.

"Our Jewish state will have a republican constitution," replied Herzl; "the monarchical principle..." and he shook his head disapprovingly.

I was struck by the way Herzl spoke of the Jewish state as though it was to come into being in the near future, as though it was an idea whose realization was in no way problematical and depended solely upon our will. His confidence flowed across to us.

"We Jews have always worked for other movements," said Herzl. "We have brought this or that 'ism' to life, and then they have always thrown us out. Now, for once, we will work for ourselves."

Two questions were flung at him from different parts of the room, almost at the same instant: "What language will be spoken in our state?" and "Will the Sabbath be kept?"

"What language?" replied Herzl. "Whichever proves itself the strongest will be spoken. The Sabbath? No one will be prevented from keeping it sacred."

". . . in our state" one of the questioners has said. He treated the Jewish state as a fact, as a tangible reality. The assurance with which Herzl discussed every detail and replied promptly and decisively to every question had cast a spell over us. We asked our questions in a spirit which, like his own, might easily have led one to believe that we were speaking of the most concrete, normal matters.

"The shortcomings of my pamphlet are its virtues," said Herzl. "Whatever is unclear will be discussed until it is clear. I wanted to provide a stimulus."

As he was about to leave, with the carriage we had sent for already waiting outside, he stopped at the door and said to the listeners gathered about him: "When we were still shut up in the ghetto, we had nothing to do but to sit over books and pedantically analyze each letter. We must give that up now. The pedantry, the hair-splitting, the squabbling must stop; we must go forward united. But"—his glance seemed directed somehow not at his listeners but at others—"if you simply must fight, if you are that foolish, then wait until you are over there, fight over there—but it would be better never to fight again, to remain united."

By "over there" Herzl plainly meant "in the Jewish state."

Then he offered a word of admonition: "You must stand on your own feet. I assume that you already think in philosophical terms. You must learn something, must read, but then you must keep your eyes open and form your own opinions."

We listened earnestly and receptively to his words. There was more than one among us who was fond of polemicizing, of heckling at club discussions. Yet, strange to relate, not one of these contentious individuals took it into his head to quibble at what Herzl said.

Herzl came, spoke and conquered.

It was as though he possessed a mysterious power, an indefinable something, which drew people under his spell. Had someone else—Chief Rabbi Güdemann perhaps—spoken to us in this way about a Jewish state, we would have been far more critical and less receptive. Reproduced here in fragmentary fashion, Herzl's words cannot possibly convey the impression they made on us when they came from his lips like a living revelation.

3

IN THE 2ND DISTRICT OF VIENNA, a section largely inhabited by Jews and known as *Leopoldstadt,* there is a small, rather quiet street called the *Rembrandtstrasse.* No. 11 *Rembrandtstrasse* housed the offices of the "Zion" Society, an organization whose full name was "Vienna Branch of the 'Zion' Union of Austrian Societies for the Colonization of Palestine and Syria."

The "Zion" Society consisted of Viennese Jewish citizens who had undertaken to promote, by word and deed, the settlement of Jewish colonists in the land of their fathers. The settlement was on a small scale and, so to speak, privately undertaken, not in the form of a Jewish state. It was the method Herzl had described as "infiltration." The Jewish colonies in Palestine and Syria, both of which were then part of the Ottoman Empire, were completely dependent on the benevolent attitude of the Turkish sovereign.

Since Herzl appeared on the scene with his idea of a Jewish state, new life had begun to stir at No. 11 *Rembrandtstrasse,* where the "Zion" Society had at times shown a tendency toward sleepy inactivity. Herzl occasionally came to the evening meetings, and the hope that "Perhaps Dr. Theodor Herzl will be there!" drew more members and guests to the "Zion" clubrooms than ever before. The atmosphere at the meetings was that of a family circle, with speeches and discussions carried on in a relaxed, informal manner. At an appropriate point, Herzl would break into the discussion and set forth his program. Thus, before long the house on the *Rembrandtstrasse* became one of the

places from which the Jewish-state concept streamed forth
·into the world.

The "Zion" evenings brought Herzl in contact with
members of the Viennese Jewish community, with mer-
chants, tradesmen, scholars, lawyers and doctors. We students, too, sometimes took part in the discussions. One
Tuesday evening, I was at my favorite haunt, the students'
club. After scanning the newspapers for a time, I proposed
to several friends: "Let's go to the *Rembrandtstrasse*. Perhaps we'll hear something interesting there."

I little suspected what consequences this casual suggestion was to have for me.

We marched off across the Danube Canal, over the
Maria Theresa Bridge, and soon found ourselves in the
modestly furnished rooms of the "Zion" Society. A delightful surprise: Herzl was there, accompanied by a
Professor Kellner. It was the third time that I had seen
him: first, at the club, when he unfurled before us his flag
with the seven stars; then in the street with his father, and
now at the "Zion" meeting. He had walked in unan-
nounced.

"The gentleman at the table next to Dr. Herzl is Professor Kellner," one of my friends whispered to me.

"What sort of a professor?" I asked.

"English language and literature."

The discussion was already in full swing; at the moment
we arrived, the conversation had got around to the subject
of Hungary—then, of course, a part of the Hapsburg Mon-
archy. The anti-Semitic ruffians who sat in the Viennese
and other Austrian legislative bodies and in the newspaper
offices were in the habit of complaining that the people of
Hungary were not sufficiently anti-Semitic; the Jews had
far too easy a time of it in that part of the Empire. As a

result, the Hungarians were referred to by the Austrian anti-Semites as the "Judeo-Magyars" and Budapest was derided as "Judapest."

I discovered a new side of Herzl's personality that evening. At the club, when he was expounding the principles of his Jewish state to us, it was the agitator in him that stood forth most prominently. Here at the "Zion," however, it was Herzl the conversationalist who sat comfortably at the long table, chatting about this subject and that in an easy, unforced manner.

In Hungary, he said, things were not quite as rosy as might appear at first glance. For example, in Budapest there was a group known as the Gentry Club, whose members came from the Hungarian nobility. Fine, respectable people. But just let a Jew—one who had been given noble rank for his services to the Empire—apply for admission to the Club. He would be certain of rejection. Herzl recounted this without indignation or emotion. Rather, he was like a scientist reporting a natural phenomenon.

Professor Kellner was the next to speak. Since the Zionist idea has taken possession of Herzl's thoughts, he declared, there had been a noticeable change in his literary contributions to the *Neue Freie Presse*. An unmistakable change for the better. The *feuilletons* had gained in substance and seriousness, and therefore had more solid merit than ever. "This is a different Herzl," the reader must be saying to himself now. And the change was clearly the result of Herzl's new preoccupation with lofty things.

I had watched Herzl while Professor Kellner delivered his eulogy. He did not move a muscle, but calmly followed the speaker's remarks as though the praise was meant not for him but for some third person. No deprecatory words, no modest protest. Encomiums doubtless meant little to him, for he had surely heard many of them; on the other hand, he was probably interested to hear an opinion about his work, whether favorable or unfavorable—particularly when it came from one versed in literature. And there may have been another reason why Herzl did not turn aside the homage paid him: Praise for the author of an idea means, in effect, praise for the idea itself. Lauding Herzl meant advancing the concept of a Jewish state. And this was precisely what Herzl wanted most to achieve.

The next speaker was a Dr. Landesberger, a lawyer. He spoke rapidly and with something of the air of a fanatic. Our first duty, our main task, he declared, was to bring Jewish culture to the Jewish masses, especially in Eastern Europe, to diffuse knowledge of the Hebrew tongue and literature. Dr. Landesberger warmed to his thesis, supported it in detail, and closed by stressing its absolute urgency.

"Herr Rosenberger has the floor," announced the chairman of the discussion. I had previously asked permission to speak. It was nothing unusual for me to make impromptu remarks at clubs and other meetings, and I suffered no pangs of stage-fright.

My subject was a rather serious one, but I tried to approach it in a good-humored manner, addressing myself in an informal fashion to the preceding speaker, Dr. Landesberger. As I spoke, I could not help noticing that Herzl was following my words with visible pleasure and an approving smile.

The gist of my brief remarks was as follows: What the suffering Jewish masses needed above all was bread. First bread, then books. Without food, one could starve to death in the finest library. *"Plenus venter non studet libenter,"* said the Latin proverb; "a full stomach does not like to study"—but an empty stomach likes to study far less. Yet, why should it be a matter of either-or? One could combine the two needs: Give the people bread and, at the same time, books. If not in Eastern Europe, then eastward from Europe, in Palestine.

I would not have reproduced these virtual commonplaces here if they had not had consequences later on.

Although it would have been an easy matter in this intimate group, I did not introduce myself to Herzl. The reason, truth to tell, was shyness. And yet I hadn't felt the slightest timidity about speaking in his presence.

There were several more speakers, who dealt with other matters. As the evening neared an end, my friends and I circled about the crowd surrounding Herzl and left.

*   *   *

In mid-February 1896 occurred an event that marked a turning point in the history of the Jewish people: the publication of Herzl's pamphlet *The Jewish State*. And, since the destinies of nations are tightly intertwined, one can say that the appearance of *The Jewish State* in the show-window of M. Breitenstein's bookstore at No. 5 *Währingerstrasse* also had its ultimate effect on the great complex of events which we call world history.

Historic events are not always heralded by the flourish of trumpets. In the case of Herzl's *The Jewish State,* its appearance was neither noisily acclaimed nor totally ignored. It was noticed and remarked upon, but few people had any notion that this 86-page pamphlet with its plain format contained more dynamism, more creative potential than all the other books in the store at No. 5 *Währingerstrasse.*

The Zionists, however, greeted Herzl's book as an ally which added substantial new strength to their ranks. The words which they had hitherto uttered only hesitantly or not at all, lest they be made to look ridiculous and dismissed as visionaries, now stood in black and white, in big, fearless Roman letters, on the title page of the pamphlet: *The Jewish State.* The full title was: *The Jewish State: An Attempt at a Modern Solution of the Jewish Problem,* by Theodor Herzl, Dr. Jur.

At first, they were only words—words which it required great courage to utter. The Zionists now had the task of transforming them into reality. And Herzl's little book marked out the path they had to follow.

4

I SOON LEARNED THAT HERZL had not forgotten my speech at the "Zion" Society. Rosenbaum of the Jewish student society "Unitas" reported to me that Herzl had told him: "That fellow Rosenberger should give propaganda speeches. He would inspire his audiences; he's a real popular orator." My friend Lerner from the *Akademische Lesehalle* reported a similar remark by Herzl.

Not long afterward, I shook hands with Herzl for the first time. As he was leaving a meeting, he extended his hand to say good-bye. I introduced myself by name. "I already know you," he said in his winning manner. "I have heard you speak."

Another time, we briefly exchanged greetings at the Ronacher Hall. The occasion was a festive evening

attended chiefly by students but also by prominent representatives of the Jewish community. I was sitting among
my comrades from the *Lesehalle,* waiting for the evening
to begin, when the word was passed from mouth to mouth:
"Herzl has arrived!" He was escorted into the hall by the
medical student I. Schalit, a member of the student society
"Kadimah."

We students rose from our seats. As Herzl came up,
looking to see who was present, he stopped in front of me,
extended his hand, and asked in a friendly way: "How are
you?" Schalit broke in: "He has just fought a mighty
battle." He was referring to a speech I had delivered not
long before at the *Lesehalle* during a debate with the
"Free Association," a Social Demoratic student club whose
spokesmen we had invited to our hall.

A greeting by Herzl, even if it was only a brief "How
are you?" was regarded among us students as a signal
honor which lent prestige to the one thus addressed. I
did not fail to note the incident down in my diary, and
some of the pleasure I felt then returns to me as I read
the entry today and as I write these lines.

And now I want to make a confession and reveal a
secret which I confided to only the very closest of my
school comrades: I wrote poetry. I had been attracted to
the Muse since early youth, and in my first semester at the
German University in Prague I had the satisfaction of
seeing my productions printed for the first time in a Berlin
magazine. In Vienna, where I continued my studies, the
Deutsches Dichterheim published my verse and some of
my small prose sketches appeared in the *Wiener Tagblatt.*

Yet, despite these successes and the appreciative letters
I had received from the editors concerned, I continued to
have gnawing doubts about my literary ability. One day,

sitting in my room, I decided to ask Herzl for his opinion. He was, after all, a prominent writer and surely qualified to judge. Accordingly, I drew two unpublished stories out of my briefcase and sent them to Herzl with a request for an appraisal.

I received a prompt reply, one which is noteworthy in more than one respect: for the advice he gives an aspiring writer, for his concept of what a writer is, and for the care with which he read the manuscripts despise the many claims on his time. The letter, written on the stationery of the *Neue Freie Presse* in a small, graceful hand without a single correction, reads as follows:

"March 26, 1897

"Dear Herr Rosenberger!

"I carefully read both of your stories because I have taken an interst in you since I heard you speak so well and skilfully. As a rule, I give no definite answer to inquiries like yours, for it is assuming a great responsibility to advise a young man either for or against a literary career. I believe you have talent, although neither of the stories is a finished product. As I read them, I reflected on what it is you lack. I believe it is the right models. We rarely or never begin with our own ideas alone. It is my impression that you have followed poor models, especially in "The Theft." It contains many tasteless passages, though the historical top-hat collection and the punch-line at the end are not bad. I find "The Unlucky One" better; it is a Mark Twain-like notion, though it becomes trite toward the end.

"My advice is thus as follows: Read, but read only proven masters. You will know who they are from the fame they enjoy after the exaggerated praise and blame of contemporaries has died away. Don't become enamored of the uncertain moderns. Seek out the simple ones; one learns most from the simple ones. Only after that should you seek yourself, and then you will find yourself.

"Above all, however, you must not neglect your serious professional studies. Whatever one studies seriously gives one the inner support that every sensible man needs in life—the writer, too. A writer, in my opinion, is nothing special—merely a more intense or, if you wish, more profound sensible man who expresses his thoughts and feelings so that they may be understood by all. *Vir bonus scribendi peritus.*

"Does this advice seem to involve too much delay? It is, to the best of my knowledge and in all good conscience, correct. If it does not quite satisfy you today, then keep this letter and in a few years you will find that I have not advised you badly. Above all, learn!

"With Zion's greetings, yours truly,

TH. HERZL

His letter, with the deep interest that it shows, moves me even today as I read it.

The phrase "historical top-hat collection" refers to a short story which I had submitted to Herzl: The protagonist of the story was an eccentric who had amassed a collection of top-hats for his own bizarre reasons.

5

FOR SEVERAL WEEKS, I SAW very little of Herzl, and then only from a distance. Then an unexpected event occurred. One Sunday in May 1897, at about 3 in the afternoon, a friend of mine named Steiner, a student at the Academy of Art, came to my modest room at No. 3 *Mosergasse.* Steiner was approximately my age; I was then 22. He was a sculptor, and I knew that he was making busts of Herzl's parents at that time. Upon entering, he told me that he had an important message to deliver. The conversation which follows is taken from the notations in my diary.

"You are bringing an important message?" I asked. "From whom?"

"Guess."

"I am not sufficiently omniscient."

My friend stretched me on the rack a bit more and then said with an air of importance: "Dr. Herzl sent me to you."

"Indeed."

"He invites you to visit him at his home in the *Berggasse.*"

I was utterly astounded: "Dr. Herzl? I am to visit him? Why?"

Steiner replied with a significant smile: "You will learn that from him."

"When shall I go?"

"Right now, if you can. I will accompany you to the front gate. It is not far from here."

My heart was pounding as I climbed the stairs at No. 6 *Berggasse.* Herzl came to meet me in his study and greeted me as though I were a good friend. He was wearing a simple gray lustring jacket. His wife sat writing at a small table by the window. I was introduced without ceremony, whereupon Herzl asked me to take a seat next to his desk. It was my impression that Frau Herzl had been informed as to why I was there.

Seating himself at the desk, Herzl offered me a cigar. When I replied that I didn't smoke, he expressed astonishment. He then set about preparing his cigar in a rather elaborate manner. I felt that he was considering how he should begin the conversation.

At last, he broke the silence: "How do you stand with your medical examinations?"

He knew, then, that I was a medical student.

"Thus far," I replied, "I have completed all the examinations on time. Five months ago, the first *Theoretikum*. Before that, the *Praktika*. In other words, the whole first *Rigorosum*."

I tried to seem at ease. In reality, I was more ill at ease during this first interview with Herzl than I would have been with anyone else.

Herzl started to talk about medical science and its services to humanity. I recalled with amusement that I had first chosen the field of medicine because, as a *Gymnasium* student, I had hoped it would be possible, with the aid of a scalpel and a microscope, to find the soul—somewhere in the brain, perhaps. Since then, I had come to realize that the matter was not so simple.

"Do you hear, Julie?" said Herzl gaily to his wife, pronouncing her name in the French manner. "He wanted to discover the soul!"

Frau Herzl looked up, nodded assent, and went on writing.

Herzl was in no hurry to get to the matter at hand. It was a leisurely conversation which offered me no hint of what he was aiming at. I was growing increasingly curious as to why he had invited me. Surely not to chat in this fashion.

He allowed occasional pauses to arise, during which he pensively sharpened a pencil or blew clouds of cigar smoke. His wife called him over to her table; he read part of the letter she was writing and made a few suggestions on how to go on, which she accepted with thanks. At last, after returning to his desk, Herzl told me the following:

He was about to start publishing a magazine, a weekly which would propagate the idea of a Jewish state and work for its realization. Dr. S. R. Landau was the executive editor, and Schalit, the medical student from the "Kadimah" society, was also a member of the editorial staff. There had been a sudden development, however. In the next few days, probably the very next day, Schalit was to leave for the Balkans as head of a group of Jewish medical students who, at the outbreak of the Greek-Turkish War, had offered their medical services to the Turkish Army.

Herzl asked me if I would like to fill in for Schalit on the magazine. He intimated that I might remain as a permanent member of the editorial staff, together with Schalit, after the latter's return. Gratified by the flattering proposal, I accepted at once.

"But you must not neglect your medical studies," said Herzl emphatically. "Schalit also had to promise me that he would be sure to prepare for his medical examinations.... Now, as to the question of salary...."

I interrupted to say that the question of money was immaterial and that the opportunity to aid our noble cause would be ample reward for me. But Herzl replied firmly that accepting my services without pay was out of the question. If I insisted on this, then we could not possibly come to terms. "The magazine might just as well not accept payment from subscribers," he argued. Hence, I agreed to take the amount that had been fixed as Schalit's salary: 40 gulden a month.

The conversation now turned to my editorial duties. "I know that you can write," said Herzl, "but you have more to learn. I want to be your adviser—but you must take my advice."

This admonition was uttered in a kindly, paternal tone. I had already become warmly attached to Herzl at this first real meeting; without intending to, he had increasingly captivated me.

He asked me next whether I had a notebook.

I drew it out of my pocket.

Could I take shorthand?

"Yes."

At this point, Frau Herzl remarked, while continuing to write: "Shorthand must stand you in very good stead."

"It certainly does," I replied. "I would have a great deal of difficulty keeping up with the lectures at the university were it not for my shorthand."

So she is following our conversation, I thought; then she is interested in the subject.

And now a few words about the impression which Frau Julie Herzl made on me at this first encounter—an impression, I might add, which further contact confirmed and I never had to revise.

6

FRAU JULIE HERZL WAS A simple, unaffected woman who had no inclination to play the great lady. Her behavior was that of a woman of the well-to-do Viennese middle class.

When I saw her for the first time in May 1897, I judged from her appearance that she was about 32, but I later learned that she had been only 29. She had a medium figure with a slight tendency toward plumpness. Looking at the Herzls, one might have said they confirmed the old adage that opposites attract: he dark-haired, she fair-haired with light-colored eyes.

With her regular features, which easily broke into a friendly smile, Frau Herzl could be described as very pretty. Her complexion was delicate, fair and flawless. She moved in a naturally composed manner, never with undue haste or agitation.

At this very first visit, I noticed that Frau Herzl was thoroughly familiar with the Jewish-state idea and with her husband's plan to publish a magazine. And her demeanor during my conversation with Herzl seemed to indicate that she sympathized with his aspirations. Several more times while we were talking, he interrupted with a "Do you hear, Julie?"

"Do you read many newspapers?" Herzl asked me at one point.

"No. . . . But I can do so from now on."

"Did you know," he inquired, "that the 'Union' recently held a meeting?"

"I was there. It was in the banquet hall of the Lower Austrian Chamber of Commerce and Industry."

He nodded. "Write a report on it."

(The "Austrian-Israelite Union" was a society of Jewish citizens who sought to protect the interests of their hard-pressed co-religionists.)

I asked Herzl what the physical appearance of the manuscript should be. He took a folia sheet of paper from the desk, folded it once lengthwise, and explained: "One half should contain writing; the other should be left blank for possible insertions and corrections. I write on the left-hand side. The back of the sheet should contain no writing." I nodded to indicate that I would follow this procedure.

Next I noted down, as Herzl gave them to me, the sections of the new magazine which I would handle: club news, a weekly calendar, a column entitled "World Chronicle." Hardly the sort of work that would require much literary talent, I thought to myself.

Not for a moment did it occur to me that I might not prove equal to the demands made on me. I took it for granted that I would quickly learn the ropes in my new journalistic pursuit.

The conversation continued a while longer, as we talked about the magazine and other matters. Finally, after arranging to meet Herzl the following morning at 8:30 or 9 at the *Wiener Mode,* I took my leave, kissing Frau Herzl's hand before I went.

The *Wiener Mode* was a fashion magazine whose printing facilities we were to use for our weekly. "Our" weekly ... I could indeed call it that now.

7

I LEFT HERZL'S HOUSE with a feeling of exhilaration. I was an editor. Just two hours before, I had walked through these same streets as an ordinary medical student —and now as an editor. Quite a step up in the world, I thought.

I had always had great respect for the position of an editor. I saw in him a man who could write whatever he pleased and see it published, who could accept or reject at his own discretion the manuscripts submitted by others.

In my case, moreover, I was an editor of a special kind. I had been favored by unusual good fortune: My editor-in-chief was Theodor Herzl. I had the joyful feeling of a military officer who is privileged to serve under a revered commander. If previously I had esteemed Herzl highly and sympathized with him, after our conversation I had become extremely attached to him. His engaging manner and the interest he showed in me had won my complete devotion. I was ready to go through fire for him.

I was uplifted by the thought that I was to be permitted to join in Herzl's work, to help build the Jewish state. Until then, I had made my modest contribution to the Jewish cause with only the spoken word. Henceforth, I hoped, I would be able to employ the written word instead and thereby exert a far wider influence.

Filled with these thoughts, I directed my steps toward the Café *Jägerhof* on the *Porzellangasse,* a favorite gathering place of Jewish students. There I found Steiner, to whom I reported the outcome of my visit to the *Berggasse*. He evidently had nothing more pressing to do than to pass the news around the café, so that on my way home soon afterward I was accompanied by a number of friends who congratulated me and prophesied all manner of good things.

Back in my room, I ruminated over what had happened. I had a suspicion that the editorial position Herzl had offered me was by no means intended to be temporary. Would he have inquired so urgently about the status of my medical examinations if he had merely meant me to interrupt my studies for a short time? And another indication: I had learned at the Café *Jägerhof* that the Jewish medical expedition was to leave the following evening for Salonika, in Turkey, and that two days earlier Schalit had received his final instructions from the Turkish Ambassador in Vienna. Consequently, Herzl had had at most two days to consider whom he would name to the editorial staff in Schalit's place; from this I might well conclude that he had not made the decision to choose me in the past day or two but had had me in mind previously.

However that might be, I now had to write the report on the "Union" which Herzl had requested. And I had better take care that it was not too sarcastic in tone.

This latter self-admonition was very much to the point. In our juvenile fashion, we students regarded the respectable Jewish citizens who made up the "Union" as "Philistines," and we were fond of appearing uninvited at their meetings and expressing our opinions with loud interruptions or even more violent demonstrations. In fact, most of these good people were anything but Philistines. But

we held it against them that, following the practice of the
Jewish community at that time, they belonged to the
Austrian Liberal party instead of sharing our faith that
Jewish salvation lay in a nationalist separatism which
aspired to create an independent Jewish commonwealth.

After completing the report, I wrote a long letter to my
parents, who lived in the town of Komotau in Bohemia,
telling them that Dr. Theodor Herzl had appointed me an
editor of his new weekly magazine. I also said I was hopeful that my medical studies would not suffer as a result.

I had a university comrade, Julius Wolf, a member
of the Jewish students society "Libanonia," who was a
sincerely devoted friend. We had worked side by side
at the dissecting table and in the laboratory, and together
we had "crammed" many a bit of medical lore for our
examinations. When I told Wolf, who was a diligent
student, about the sudden turn of ovents, he shook his
head anxiously: "And your *Rigorosen?* Your medical
studies?"

"I'll manage them all right," I replied confidently.

"Do you think so?"

"Of course!"

"I'm not so sure," he said, shaking his head once more.
"Take care that you don't idle away your time in joural-
ism, so that all the work you've already done is lost—
together with your doctor's degree."

8

THE MORNING FOLLOWING MY interview with Herzl, Monday May 31, I started out for the *Wiener Mode,* where our weekly was to be printed. Riding on the trolley, I wondered whether Herzl would be satisfied with my work. He had, so to speak, taken a chance on me, making me his editorial colleague without really knowing me—a mark of confidence for which he as yet had no real basis. I resolved not to disappoint him.

The name of our magazine was to be *Die Welt* ("The World"). What would it look like? What format would it have? Big, small, thick, thin? Herzl had not said a word on the subject.

I admired the single-minded energy which had led Herzl to found the new magazine. The second stage on the road to the Jewish state! The first stage, or rather the starting point, had been the book, *The Jewish State.* Now there was *Die Welt* to open the way for a further advance. In today's world, the written word was truly a fighter in the front lines.

At 8:30, I arrived at the *Wiener Mode,* where I was told that Herzl was on the second floor. I found him in the office of Herr Steiner, general manager of the fashion magazine. Herzl introduced me.

Steiner was a man of 38, though his beard made him appear older. Of less than medium height, he expressed himself fluently and was agile in his movements. I was struck by the way he trilled his R in the manner of the stage. He was a recent convert to our cause who had been fired by Herzl's example and also by his book. (Under the name "York Steiner," he was to a contributor of *Die Welt*.)

As soon as Steiner had left, Herzl asked:

"Did you bring the report on the 'Union' meeting?"

I handed him the manuscript. He read it, slowly and searchingly, then looked at me and said, "It's good."

Then he took his blue pencil and began to strike out lines. (In my diary, I find the observations that he struck out more than was necessary. Today, I strongly suspect that he knew what he was doing.) As I watched with interest, he deleted parts and linked up what was left with short transitions. The result of this operation, a mixed product of two authors, appeared in the first issue of the magazine in the column headed "The Week."

After editing my report, Herzl picked up a long strip of paper which contained printed matter in the form of a newspaper column.

"You can be very helpful here," he said. "I am about to read the galley proofs."

Noting my questioning look, he added: "Do you know what a galley proof is?"

I confessed that I didn't.

"Take a look," said Herzl, pointing to strips of paper still wet with ink. "They're preliminary impressions of the type. We have to read them for typographical errors before the final printing.... Do you know how to read proof?"

Again I had to say no.

Herzl was neither surprised nor disappointed. "I'll show you. Read it with me.... There's a 'typo' already. You strike out the incorrect letter with a special mark—thus!—and write the correct one in the margin next to the mark—thus!"

In a patient, friendly manner, like a kindly teacher instructing a pupil, Herzl initiated me into the technical rudiments of my new work. Then he went down to the printshop to give some instructions. When he returned, he found that I had succeeded in botching a whole galley proof: Not satisfied with merely making the correct letter in the margin, I had written the entire word. Herzl sat down and transferred the corrections himself, in the proper form, to the other margin. When he noticed that I was somewhat embarrassed by my awkwardness, he said in a friendly way: "It doesn't matter. You'll learn how to do it." He acted more like a friend than like a "boss." Indeed, during all the time I worked with him, I never heard him utter an unfriendly or peevish word.

Yet, I felt very shy with him that day. Why? I can think of no adequate explanation. Herzl certainly did nothing to make me feel that way. On the contrary, he was the very soul of friendliness. Was it "force of personality?" That is an expression that really explains nothing. The fact is, I was not the only one who had ever lost a bit of his customary aplomb in Herzl's presence. I had seen both young and old act self-conscious with him. My friend Isaak Lerner, who was approximately my age, once said to me: "When I am in Herzl's presence, I feel like a child."

Herzl gave me some additional pointers for my work that first day at the *Wiener Mode*. The galley proof on which I made my first corrections is still in my possession. Obviously, even in those very first days, I felt a desire to preserve papers which bore a few marks in Herzl's handwriting or which, through their association with him, conjured up memories for me.

The galley proofs of *Die Welt* were curious-looking, to say the least. They had previously served as "galleys" for the *Wiener Mode,* and consequently they contained all manner of illustrations and text from that periodical on the reverse side. Thus, on the back of the historic galley already referred to, I noticed a picture of a "head-cushion in Gobelin satin-stitch" and an article on the linen trousseau of a Vienese upper-class family. Type which had sung the praises of an "English walking and visiting dress of dark-blue braided material" was used two days later to proclaim a serious political program. Hidden behind the galley of a piece of heavy polemics by Max Nordau is a pretty young *Wienerin,* wearing a hat in the current fashion piled high with flowers, feathers and ribbon-loops; the young lady obviously has no idea what is going on behind her back.

*   *   *

Herzl's speaking voice was baritone. I could not possibly imagine his otherwise—with a clear, thin tenor or a booming bass. His voice, of pleasantly medium range and an even, modulated strength, was an inseparable part of his personality. Indeed, it was one of the qualities that made him attractive.

His mode of speech and his pronunciation were unaffected and free of any trace of dialect. His spoken German gave no clue as to his geographical origins; it was the pure yet unforced German in use among cultivated people wherever the language enjoyed currency. At home, Herzl's wife and children spoke the same "normal German."

9

THE GREAT DAY HAD COME: the birthday of *Die Welt*. The first issue of Herzl's magazine appeared on Friday, June 4, 1897.

Public reaction was much like that which had greeted the publication of *The Jewish State*. *Die Welt* caused comment, even though it did not create a great sensation. It was received with varied emotions in different places. "What does this magazine want? A Jewish state? A state consisting only of Jews from its chief down to the lowliest shepherd? Ah!" And which intonation this "Ah!" possessed depended on whether it came from the mouth of a "liberal" Jew or a Zionist or an anti-Semite.

Many had supposed that the popular light author Theodor Herzl would abandon the Jewish theme after that peculiar aberration, the *Jewish State* pamphlet, and return to writing beautiful, innocuous, completely non-political *feuilletons*. They were disappointed and astonished when *Die Welt* made its appearance. So he was serious, deadly serious, that strange man! He meant to pursue the matter, to continue riding his hobby-horse—in fact, judging from all appearances, to turn the hobby-horse into a real war-horse. For proof, one had only to read the "Program" which he announced on the first page of his new weekly. There he said:

"Our weekly is a 'Jewish paper.'

"We mean to take this expression, which is used as a term of abuse, and turn it into one of honor.

"*Die Welt* is a paper for Jews. For which Jews? For the
strong, who receive help anyway? No, they do not need
support.

"*Die Welt* is a paper for the poor, the weak, the young,
but also for all those who, while themselves not suffering
affliction, have found their way home to their race. Let
no one dare to say that we are fanning class hatred among
Jews when we concern ourselves with our weaker brothers.
There are men enough in our ranks who are neither
'Proletarians' nor revolutionists nor hotheads. The cause
we serve is great and noble, a work of peace, a solution of
the Jewish problem which will bring reconciliation. An
idea capable of inspiring nobler human beings, whether
they be Christians, Mohammedans or Israelites.

"We wish—in the words which are already familiar to
our friends—to create a homeland that is secured by
international law for those Jews who cannot or do not
want to assimilate in their present places of residence.

"We rally under the flag of Zion. Yet, though our eyes
are fixed on a distant goal, we cannot and shall not ignore
the present-day conditions of the Jews. *Die Welt* will
serve the Jewish people as a sword and buckler—yes, and
an unsullied sword. Against whom? Against its enemies
—without regard to religion. . . ."

This was the tenor of Harzl's program, which occupied
the entire first page of *Die Welt* and concluded with the
sentence:

"*Die Welt* will be the organ of those men who wish to
lead the Jewish people upward from this era into better
times."

The program was signed: "Editorial staff of *Die Welt*."
It was appropriate, for Herzl was the editorial staff:
editor-in-chief, publisher and owner all in one.

To the Zionists and many other Jews, the program sounded like the sort of manifesto one plasters on the walls in times of unrest and peril. This undertone which Herzl had imparted to his proclamation was most timely, for anti-Semitism was busily at work and Israel was once more assailed by enemies.

Herzl's outstanding literary ability was a great asset in his mission of re-establishing a Jewish state. No other Jew or even Jewish writer of that time could have framed the *Welt* "Program" in such effective language. Herzl was a master of words, endowed with the gift of expressing what he thought and felt so that it conquered the minds and hearts of others. Among the many qualities which predestined Herzl for his role, his literary skill occupied an important place.

*   *   *

After the first issue of *Die Welt* had seen the light of day, our office was moved from the *Wiener Mode* to Herzl's home. For hours and for days at a time, I sat with him in his study in the house at No. 6 *Berggasse*: Herzl at his desk, I at an adjoining table. The work of helping to prepare the succeeding issues was enjoyable and easy, for Herzl made it so. Never did he don the formal robes of Editor-in-Chief or make one painfully conscious of his superiority. There was no trace of self-important aloofness. I always had the feeling that he was a fatherly friend who had my best interests at heart. (Herzl was then 37 and I was 22—a gap which, at my age, might well have seemed formidable enough to justify thinking of him as fatherly.) Those were wonderful days which rank among the happiest of my life.

In addition to the private, unofficial editorial office on the *Berggasse,* we had an official address which was listed on the title page of *Die Welt*: Vienna, II., No. 11 *Rem-brandtstrasse*. That was, of course, the headquarters of the "Zion" Society, where I had made the speech that proved so fateful for me. Our magazine, particularly the business department, enjoyed the use of the premises as an indefinite guest.

Herzl was an early riser. By the time I entered his study each morning between 8 and 8:30, he was sitting at his desk, a pen or pencil in his hand, his mind already preoccupied with matters pertaining to Judaism, to the Jewish state, to *Die Welt*. Once, when we were talking about a man who was known for sleeping until 10 in the morning and even later, Herzl said: "Mark my words, Rosenberger; a man who does not rise early will never amount to anything."

My work at this time consisted of getting material for *Die Welt*'s announcements column ready for the printer, reading galley proofs, and transcribing from my steno-graphic notes and the letters Herzl dictated to me. (Since we did not have a typewriter then, to say nothing of a dictaphone, pen and ink constituted our principal writ-ing materials.) The letters were replies to Jewish indi-viduals and organizations which had appealed to Herzl, as the unchallengeable authority, on matters concerning the Zionist idea.

In the course of the morning, Frau Herzl usually paid us a short visit. She would come in, wearing an ordinary house dress, with a friendly smile on her face, which sometimes showed just a trace of rice-powder. After asking her husband how he was and exchanging a few words with him, she would return to the other part of the house.

I still remember very clearly how on one occasion Frau Herzl stepped up behind her husband, who was sitting erect at his desk. "Why does everyone like you so much?" she asked tenderly and then slowly pressed a kiss on the little spot where the crown of his head had begun to show through his otherwise thick hair.

10

"GO TO THE CAFE CENTRAL and read all the newspapers. Whatever interests you interests me as well."

Herzl directed this little injunction at me one day, not long after the appearance of the first issue of *Die Welt,* as I was about to leave shortly before noon. As I noted in an earlier chapter, our magazine had a column entitled "World Chronicle" which recorded events pertaining to Jews and Judaism all over the world. Herzl's words meant that I should gather some current material for the "Chronicle."

"Whatever interests you interests me as well." Herzl was never stinting with compliments. He enjoyed making others happy by saying something pleasant. He was not one of those people who can never bring themselves to utter a word of praise because they envy others the pleasure it gives even though they themselves bestowed it.

Nor could I myself ever complain for lack of complimentary comments. The day before, in Herzl's study, I had been reading a manuscript written in such an obscure, rhetorical style that at times it verged on sheer gibberish.

Finally, I confessed aloud: "To be quite frank, I don't understand this." Herzl thereupon said: "Rosenberger, if there is someone you do not understand, then *he* is at fault, not you." To be sure, I took remarks like this with a grain of salt, as they were doubtless meant to be taken.

At all events, I now made for the Café Central, notebook and pencil in pocket, and plunged into the mass of newspapers there. The Central, at No. 14 *Herrengasse,* was one of Vienna's best-known coffee houses. Its large supply of newspapers and magazines, both Austrian and foreign, made it a favorite haunt of journalists, writers, artists, correspondents of foreign periodicals, politicians, diplomats, and intellectuals of every sort, including some Bohemian types. Chess matches were held in the side rooms, and there was also billiard tables.

Henceforth, I spent a good many hours at a marble table in the big, columned café, a newspaper in my hand and a mountain of others beside me. I soon acquired the knack of rapidly scanning the pages until my chronicler's eye lighted upon an appropriate item, and I even fell into the habit of doing much of my writing at the Central.

Herzl was no café habitué. While other Viennese writers and artists had their favorite coffee houses and their round tables, where matters great and small were discussed and literary or artistic cliques were formed, he kept away from this milieu. Indeed, what would he have done there? Surely not read newspapers. The *Neue Freie Presse,* of whose editorial staff he was a distinguished member, was delivered to his home each day, and it was a well-informed paper which provided all the most important news. He read it each morning, fairly rapidly as a rule without any consuming interest, and then handed it to me, usually without comment. If he felt the desire to look at other papers, they were available in the afternoon at the offices of the *Neue Freie Presse.*

Another reason for avoiding the coffe houses was that they consumed time, and that was a commodity of which Herzl made increasingly sparing use. The convivial coffee-house atmosphere was also well suited to the striking up of acquaintances, and Herzl had no desire to expose himself to approaches by strangers.

Neither did he wish to join any of the coffee-house cliques. As a celebrated writer, he had no need of the logrolling techniques by which the various café brotherhoods sought to promote their members' interests. Moreover, he found these methods distasteful.

While working, Herzl did not spend every minute at his desk. At times, he would get up, walk over to the corner window and, half concealed by the curtain, look down into the street. Sometimes, he stood there silently; on other occasions, he commented good-humoredly on the passing scene. "There goes one of the greatest rogues in all Vienna," he said to me once, taking further cover behind the curtain. I remained at my table, although I would very much liked to see what one of the greatest rogues in all Vienna looked like.

Another time, Herzl remarked, "There goes * * *" and named a Viennese writer and journalist. "Recently, he boasted to me that he could not speak a word of French." Then he added in amusement: "Now that's really something to boast about!" With that, Herzl returned to his desk and plunged his pen once more into the ink-well.

In the course of our work together, I became familiar with the guiding principles which Herzl had laid down for his magazine. I also gained insight into his thinking from the letters which he dictated to me. To the letters which had come from all sides following publication of *The Jewish State* were now added others addressed to the Editor of *Die Welt*, all of which Herzl read and, when necessary, answered.

Although I had not completely overcome my original shyness with Herzl, I never held back when my opinions differed from his. Herzl was not the type of opinionated person who fears a loss of prestige if he is shown to be in error. In fact, he was pleased when someone else had an opinion of his own and expressed it. Since he was far from regarding himself as infallible, he readily deferred to another's position when it was sound.

Once, I was taking down Herzl's reply to the editor of a Jewish paper that was unfriendly, in fact hostile, toward the Jewish-state idea. The paper had suggested an ex-change subscription with *Die Welt*. Suddenly, Herzl stopped dictating and asked: "Don't you approve of the reply?"

I remarked that it was a bit too brusque.

"Good," he said. "Then draft a more polite one for me."

The next day, I brought him my version. He read it and laughed heartily: "You call that more polite? That's a downright rude letter!"

The reply went off as Herzl originally dictated it.

(The adjective Herzl applied to my proposed letter was *saugrob*, a word which literally meant "rude as a hog" and was used in the Alpine region of Austria. In private conversation, he was not averse to using earthy, colloquial expressions which would have been strangely incongruous in one of his sensitively written *feuilletons*.)

Opposition, whether in private or in a public hall, did not displease Herzl. Indeed, he welcomed it, provided that

his perceptive eye did not detect an unworthy motive in
it, such as a mere desire to contradict, pomposity, carping
criticism, envy, and similar things which so often mas-
querade as "opposition." At the same time, there were
points of principle, deeply felt conviction, on which he
would brook no contradiction. There were limits to his
conciliatoriness.

In the time we spent together, I came to know Herzl
better and better. And the better I understood this extraordinary man, the more warmly attached to him I
became.

II

AT HERZL'S HOME, I BECAME
acquainted with the Reverend
Hechler, chaplain of the British Embassy in Vienna. Then
52, he was a man of medium height, rather slender, and of
an almost youthful vigor. A white beard, which reached
to his chest, lent a priestly dignity to his ruddy, blue-eyed
countenance. He spoke perfect German, with almost no
trace of an accent. Friendly in manner he went about with
a vaguely mysterious air which seemed to say, "I know of
things which are to come, to reveal themselves, which will
soon be here. . . ."

Occasionally, he drew the curtain back somewhat from
his secret by reaching into a capacious inside pocket in
his long, black lustring jacket and producing a narrow
roll of paper, a meter in length. On it, in a closely written
hand and in ink of various colors, was a table of Biblical

dates and other compuations which proved that the Jewish
people stood at a turning point in its history, at the thresh-
old of great events. It could be calculated from the Bible
that the lustrum, or five-year period, through which we
were then passing—1897 and the four preceding years—
was decisive for the fulfilment of the Biblical prophecies,
for Israel's return to Palestine, for the resurrection of the
Jewish Kingdom.

"There, check it yourself. . . ." And Hechler would point
out the figures with a curiously shaped silver pencil and
set forth his interpretation. He was firmly convinced that
these numbers bore witness to the most unimpeachable
truth. . . . And, for that matter, have later events refuted
him?

Before me are three large manuscript pages, in Hechler's hand and edited by Herzl with a blue-pencil. Hechler's own comments are written in red ink, quotations and
other important material in black ink. The quotations
show the author's intimate knowledge of the Bible.

The manuscript is that of an article by Hechler which
appeared in the second issue of *Die Welt* and created a
great stir. Here was the chaplain of the British Embassy
in Vienna demanding the establishment of a Jewish state
in Palestine! And he advanced the idea openly, without
mincing any words.

Among other things, Hechler said in his article:

"As a Christian, I also believe in the Jewish national
movement known as 'Zionism,' for according to the Bible,
indeed according to the old Hebrew prophet himself, a
'Jewish state' must arise once more in Palestine, and it
seems to me, judging from the signs of the times, that the
Jews will soon have their very own home again in their

ancient fatherland which was given them by God. May the cry soon be heard: *'Palestine for the Jews!'*

"Never forget that Almight God gave the Promised Land to Abraham and his children *for ever*.

" 'For all the land which thou seest, to thee will I give it, and to they seed for ever.'—Genesis (First Book of Moses) 13:15."

In another place, Hechler said:

"If we now add to 637 or 638 the 1260 years during which Jerusalem was trampled under foot, we obtain the year *1897 or 1898*.

"The inference is that, if we have thus discovered the divinely ordained beginning of the long-prophesied trampling-down of Jerusalem, we must now be in the era of the Jews' return to Palestine. The immediate future will show whether this calculation and explanation of the Biblical prophecy is correct. Of this I am certain: If now is the divinely ordained time for the Jews' return to Palestine, no power will be able to prevent the carrying out of God's will."

Hechler concluded by saying:

"What does all this prove? That I, as a believing Christian, must believe that the Jews will once more return to Palestine and found a new Jewish state, for it is written thus in the word of God, and God wills it. Let that be your motto! *God wills it!*....

"Ye children of Abraham, awake! God himself, the Heavenly Father, calls you back to your ancient fatherland and wants to be your God.

"And may this God of Abraham, Isaac and Jacob bless you with heavenly blessings beyond all prayer and understanding and add many more to your blessings, as He promised of old through his prophets.

   "Vienna, June 4, 1897.

WILLIAM HENRY HECHLER,
Chaplain to Her Britannic Majesty's
Embassy in Vienna."

Hechler saw in Herzl, if not actually the prophesied Jewish Messiah, then at least the herald who announces the approach of the messianic kingdom. And yet, judging from some of his remarks, he may have had moments when he really did regard Herzl as the Messiah sent by God.

These messianic ideas of Hechler rested on a realistic foundation: First a Zion had to arise—not the imaginary, other-worldly Jerusalem, but an earthy Zion, with inhabitants of flesh and blood, a Jewish state in Palestine. And this restoration of the Jewish state, foretold by Holy Scripture, would be the sign, the dawn that announced that the great messianic day had come here on earth for all mankind.

This was Hechler's thinking. And he regarded Herzl as the instrument chosen by Providence to carry out this messianic design. Once, he said to me in his mysterious way:

"He is living among us . . . the King . . . incognito . . . but it does not conceal him . . . the King of the Jews."

He nodded meaningfully; the reference, of course, was to Herzl. He had uttered the words "the King of the Jews" very softly as though they were so dangerous that they might bring a crown of thorns in their wake.

In personal contact with Herzl, Hechler expressed through neither word nor deed his conviction that "Thou art the Messiah, the anointed of the Lord." They maintained the simple, friendly relations of two men striving toward a common goal.

Hechler's mind was nourished by the Bible, and it was the Bible which had brought him to Herzl's Jewish-state movement. To him, it was in the most exalted sense the Book of Books, Holy Scripture, the word of God. Each word was sacred, and "Bible criticism" merely made him shrug his shoulders. He carried the Bible not only in his hand but in his heart.

The secret language of the Bible had revealed to Hechler that the period around 1897 would be a fateful one for Israel. And, indeed, the year 1896 had brought an epoch-making book, Herzl's *Jewish State,* and the year 1897 a remarkable magazine which called upon the Jews to return to the East, a magazine with a six-pointed star which was like a lodestar to the promised haven.

In his article, the Reverend Hechler bade *Die Welt* welcome in moving words which were addressed to Herzl:

"I greet with joy the appearance of the first issue of the international Zionist magazine, *Die Welt.*

"... I pray that you and your collaborators in this wonderful movement may receive the most abundant heavenly blessing of Almighty God, who governs all according to his will."

Hechler visited us occasionally at our office, and some suspicious souls thought at first that he might have missionary aims in view. However, this proved quite untrue. In my many conversations with Hechler, he never made the slightest attempt to raise religious issues with a view to converting me. His interest lay only in the Zionist goal, in establishing the Kingdom of Israel. Only occasionally did he intimate that his hopes transcended this goal and that he regarded the founding of a Jewish state in the

Holy Land as the essential first link in a wonderful chain of events which would redeem mankind.

Through his connections with highly placed individuals, particularly the Grand Duke of Baden, Hechler rendered very valuable services to the Jewish-state idea and to Herzl. He was a sincere friend of the Jews, whom he regarded as the Chosen People, the People of God. "Wonderful are God's ways with Israel, his ancient people of the covenant!" he wrote in *Die Welt*. A man of idealistic purpose, Hechler believed unshakably and longingly in the divinely ordained emergence of a Jewish state, and he was self-sacrificing in his efforts to help bring it about.

12

HERZL WAS DEEPLY ATTACHED to his three children, Pauline, Trude and Hans; he would sometimes press his lips almost reverently on Pauline's golden hair. It was distressing to him that the press of work kept him from devoting as much time to the children as he would have liked.

Pauline, the oldest, and Hans resembled their mother more; Trude looked like her father. Besides Frau Herzl, who watched over them with loving care, the children had a governess, a hard-working, devoted spinster of indeterminate age who also helped her mistress around the house. In the Herzl home, she was almost like a member of the family.

My first impression of the Herzl household was confirmed as time went on. It gave one the feeling of a well-

ordered, securely established, well-to-do home of the upper
middle class—a home where peace and harmony reign and
care does not enter.

I became acquainted with Herzl's father, Jacob, at our
business office at No. 11 *Rembrandtstrasse.* During this
early period of *Die Welt,* he had charge of the magazine's
business affairs.

I do not recall that the younger Herzl ever showed any
great interst in administrative details. Looking back on
those years, in fact, I would say that he was anything but
a "good businessman." He was not one to join the pursuit
of mammon, and, had Fortune ever dumped inordinate
riches in his lap, he would have used it for only two purposes: to finance the restoration of the Jewish state and
to make himself economically independent so that he
could devote all his energy to that same end.

Jacob Herzl, then 62, was somewhat shorter than his
son, but heavier, and seemed to be of a sound constitution.
He spoke very little and then slowly and reflectively in a
friendly but not effusive manner. As became his age, his
movements were rather deliberate.

When it was necessary, the elder Herzl would spend a
few hours in the morning checking the day's mail, the
subscription list and the bookkeeping. When editorial
duties brought me to the *Rembrandtstrasse,* I would have
an opportunity to chat with him. I thought I saw Herzl's
likeness in his father's face. Later, it seemed to me that
he looked more like his mother. And finally, as so often
happens, I came to see a family resemblance in all three.

Jacob Herzl was understandably proud of his Theodor,
even though he was not demonstrative in showing it. The
son was affectionately devoted to his parents, and the latter
had the greatest admiration for his outstanding gifts.

Herzl's father warmly sympathized with his son's Zionist strivings. Once he recalled from Theodor's youth: "When he was still very young, the rabbis predicted: 'Something great will come of him.'"

On one occasion, the *Neue Freie Presse* published a *feuilleton* by Herzl that was gay and almost frolicsome in tone. Jacob Herzl pointed it out to me and said happily: "That's the old Herzl!" Naively, I asked whether Herzl's contributions to the *Presse* were subject to editorial censorship. "What do you mean!" replied his father, astounded "What do you mean! Make cuts in an article by Theodor Herzl...!"

I still have letters sent to me by Jacob Herzl, which show his lively, detailed interest in *Die Welt's* administrative affairs. I imagine, too, that he contributed his bit financially to the magazine, for it meant a great deal to him to stand by his beloved son.

In his *feuilleton,* "The Eyeglasses," Herzl related how on one occasion the image of his father appeared suddenly before his mind's eye: "I saw my father, saw the gesture with which he took his pincenez from his upper left-hand vest pocket before beginning to read...." Thinking back, I have an equally vivid recollection of this characteristic gesture of the dignified old gentleman who was Theodor Herzl's father.

*   *   *

In those days, beards were still very much in fashion, and men of every age and class could garnish chin, jowl and upper lip to their hearts' content. Herzl's hair and beard were black; at the time I met him, he did not have a single white hair. His hair was generally straight though with some tendency toward waviness. It was combed back from the forehead, was somewhat bushy in front, and was cropped more and more closely as it approached the neck.

Herzl's head was flawlessly formed, with no irregularities to mar its rounded contour. His forehead was finely etched with lines which seemed almost to suggest the lofty thoughts beneath. His complexion was tanned-looking rather than fair, though not excessively so. His nose was well formed, slightly curved and fairly prominent, but not "fleshy." In the interest of historical accuracy be it said that it was not a "Jewish nose"—the term Herzl himself applied to it in his *Diaries*.

*   *   *

It says in the Bible, in the 9th Chapter of the Book of Samuel: "Now there was a man of Benjamin whose name was Kish, the son of Abiel. . . . And he had a son whose name was Saul, a choice young man, and a goodly: and there was not among the children of Israel a goodlier person than he: from his shoulders and upward he was higher than any of the people." Herzl may not have been a head taller "than any of the people," but he was a tall man, nevertheless, whose stature contributed to the impression he made on others. He always held his well-proportioned body erect, yet relaxed. His movements were controlled; he was not given to exaggerated gestures. Like everyone, he had his characteristic manner of walking, but it would be difficult to describe it in words. I see it clearly as I write, and yet I can only say that it was free of anything suggesting affectation or studied gravity of demeanor.

Herzl's full, black beard helped to lend a somewhat somber appearance to his face. In the early years, it was only an appearance and was belied by his cheerful, optimistic nature. Between Herzl's dark, fairly pronounced eyebrows were two short, parallel folds. Photographers were in the habit of retouching and often completely obliterating these two lines, which were really an integral part of Herzl's appearance; they performed a similar operation on the folds which ran from each side of his nose to the corners of his mouth. In so doing, they merely made the pictures which have come down to us less lifelike.

13

ON PAGE TWO of *Die Welt's* first issue, boldly signed "Dr. Theodor Herzl," appeared an announcement which astounded many readers and was received with much shaking of heads.

"A strange fellow," said some. "Now he wants to call a congress, an assembly of Jews from all parts of the world. And for what purpose? To decide upon the best ways and means for creating a Jewish state. A congress the like of which has never been seen! The man has most curious ideas. But watch, it will never come about—and, if it does, it will disgrace itself and end in a miserable fiasco."

Such was the forecast of enemies and doubters.

Since the first days I worked with Herzl, I had heard him speak of the Zionist congress, of his plan for a parliament of the dispersed children of Israel which would hold periodic brief sessions. The first congress was to meet in Munich in late August 1897, and Herzl was able to announce in issued no. 1 of *Die Welt*: "Delegates have already been named from most of the countries of Europe, as well as from Asia and Africa, and the campaign to send people to the congress has gotten off to a splendid start in the United State of America."

How easily that reads, and yet how hard Herzl had had to work before he could announce those results! What a multitude of letters he had sent off to the countries of Europe and other parts of the world! And he had had to do it all himself, with no one else to lean on.

Just as the original idea of convoking the congress had been Herzl's alone, so too he assumed the entire burden of carrying it out. Headquarters of the whole undertaking was his study at No. 6 *Berggasse;* the motor which powered it was his head. Nor was it a noisy, clangorous motor. Day after day, in moments snatched from his work for *Die Welt,* I saw him sitting quietly writing the innumerable letters to future participants in the congress. Some he wrote out himself; others he dictated to me.

Herzl was moving methodically forward. To the two instruments he had already created, his pamphlet *The Jewish State* and his magazine *Die Welt,* was to be added a third: the congress. His mighty pen was to be reinforced by a parliamentary body which would serve as a bridge to actual deeds.

He said to me once during these preparations for the congress: "The congress's time sequence is reversed.... The universal rule is: First the state exists and then its parliament is chosen. We do it the other way around: First the parialment is founded and then the state."

Another time, he said: "We are partly anticipating the Jewish state by providing it now with a parliament."

But these paradoxical elements did not trouble him at all. His point of view was: A paradox is a paradox only until it becomes a reality—and then it ofen becomes a platitude. We are flying in the face of logic? A tangible fact is stronger than any logic. As soon as the Jewish parliament has become a fact, all dialectical objections will cease. Let us create that fact.

Herzl's plan to call a congress aroused concern among a good many Zionists. It was a risky business. Who could say if it would end in success or failure? Even Herzl was uneasy at times, though his purpose remained unshaken. In conversations with me, he occasionally remarked that the congress was a gamble. Failure would damage the Zionist movement, give its enemies cause for malicious joy, and discredit the whole Jewish-state idea.

Would all the prospective delegates actually be able to keep the promises they had made in their letters to Herzl? When the time came, would they be able to make the rather lengthy trip to the congress site? Rabbi S. Schaffer of Baltimore; W. I. Temkin, the rabbi and engineer from Yelizavetgrad, Russia; Dr. Leon Wilenski of Kremenchug, Russia; Dr. D. Alcalay, the lawyer from Belgrade; Professor Belkowski of Sofia; Adam Rosenberg of New York; Dr. Joseph Seligmann of Stockholm—would they and all the others from near and far really take part?

And if the congress did take place, would its deliberations, proceeding in the full light of publicity, take a course that would fill us with pride? Or would irresponsible elements introduce a discordant note that would jar with the dignity and high purpose of the occasion and degrade the Jewish parliament in the eyes of the world? We all felt that the success or failure of the congress would mean a great deal for the future of the Zionist

Photograph of THEODOR HERZL, inscribed:
"To my dear friend and collaborator, ERWIN ROSENBERGER,
in memory of the pre-historic times of The World."

DR. ERWIN ROSENBERGER *in the year 1903*

Dr. Erwin Rosenberger *in 1959*

Meinem lieben Freund und Mitarbeiter Erwin Rosenberger

Zur Erinnerung an manche schwere Anfangsstunde.

Unser Käthchen.

März 99

Lustspiel in 4 Acten

Th Herzl

von

Theodor Herzl.

Copyright.

Wien, 1899.

Buchdruckerei „Industrie", Wien, VIII., Schlößelgasse 11.

Title page of HERZL's comedy "OUR KATHY," *inscribed:*
"To my dear friend and collaborator Erwin Rosenberger
in memory of some difficult first moments
March 1899. TH. HERZL."

„Die X Welt"
Redaction und Administration
Wien,
11. Kronprinzstraße 11.

Juli
den 26 VII 1897

Lieber Rosenberger,

in Eile, ich glaube es ist kein
zweiter Artikel da. Lassen Sie
in diesem Falle Ihren Budapester
Brief unter dem Titel ~~~~~~
„ungarische Stimmungen,"
Budapest im Juli als zweiten
Artikel setzen. Dann geben
Sie den NewYorker Brief hinter
den ungarischen Stimmungen.
Nur wenn Klötzl Männchen
macht, dass es nicht fertig
werden könne, lassen Sie
Läufers Rave als zweiten
Artikel setzen (mit Ihren
Rectificationen)
Morgen muss alles so ein-
getheilt werden, dass kein

Letter from THEODOR HERZL *to* ERWIN ROSENBERGER
Dated July 26, 1897

Uebersatz bleibt, weil wir
die nächste Nummer schon bei
Schöler haben.
Feuilleton ist marmorrtes Bauernhaus
Morgen mehr

herzlichen Gruss
von Ihrem
Herzl

Geben Sie auf Rülfs Schluss
acht, den ich nicht im
Abzug erhielt. Streichen
Sie eventuell seine
Unvorsichtigkeiten.

Continuation of HERZL's *letter of July 26, 1897.*

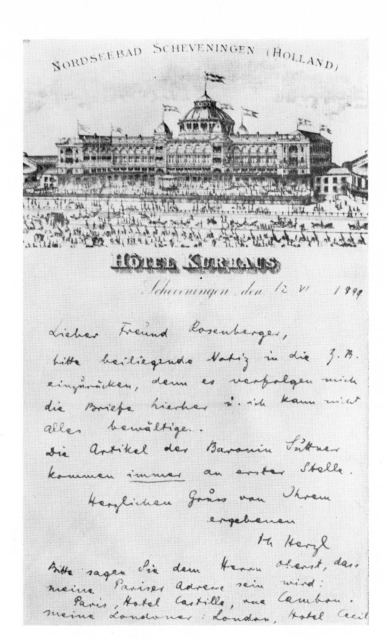

Letter from THEODOR HERZL to ERWIN ROSENBERGER
Dated June 12, 1899

„Die Welt"
Redaction und Administration
Wien
IX., Turkenstrasse 9

Wien den *21. IX* 190 *3*

Mein lieber Rosenberger,

Beschwerdekästchen" ausge-
zeichnet! Fahren Sie fort,
aber lustig!

Ihr getreuer

Herzl

Letter from HERZL *to* ROSENBERGER
Dated September 21, 1903

movement. And we wished it well as fervently as our adversaries wished it ill.

One of the goals which Herzl advanced in his "Program" in the first issue of *Die Welt* was "emigration of the Jewish masses to the land of their fathers." In Tsarist Russia at that time, there were nearly six million Jews, barely existing under the most wretched conditions, oppressed, deprived of all rights, and constantly threatened by the Damoclean sword of pogroms. The pogrom was an unofficial state institution; whenever the Russian ruling class felt threatened by popular discontent or ferment of any sort, it diverted the people's fury in another direction—against the Jews. There the fury would burn itself out, and the regime could feel safe once again.

In Rumania, 300,000 Jews fared little better. In Galicia, then a province of Austria, some 800,000 Jews lived for the most part in abject poverty. And in various sections of Western and Central Europe, especially in the German-speaking parts of Austria, the Jews had a special function: Whenever an ambitious demagogue wished to launch a political career, he had only to inscribe a few anti-Semitic slogans on his banner and he was assured of a popular following. When Herzl created the new Zionist movement and set about preparing for the congress, he hoped that by returning to the land of their fathers the Jewish masses could be rescued from this role of political scapegoat and from their life of misery.

And now let us turn to a man who played a significant part in Herzl's life and in the Jewish-state movement, a man who was Herzl's friend and collaborator. He was ten years older than Herzl, was born in Budapest like the latter, and was also a noted writer—indeed, one of even greater renown. Thickset and shorter than Herzl, bearded

like him, he radiated nobility of mind and had the power
to capture an audience. His name was Max Nordau, and
he published an article in *Die Welt*'s second issue, dated
June 11, 1897, which produced a sensation.

14

MAX NORDAU'S ARTICLE WAS
a sensation less because of its con-
tent—even though this did attract considerable attention—
than because of the identity of its world-renowned author.
Many could not believe their own eyes. Had a man like
Nordau really gone over to the Zionists? Had he, too,
taken up the cudgels for a Jewish state? Obviously, he
had—quite publicly, in a lead article in issue no. 2 of *Die
Welt*. And he was to remain true in his allegiance to his
friend Herzl through all the later phases of the Zionist
movement.

In his article, Nordau turned all his polemical skill
against the Chief Rabbi of Vienna, Dr. Moritz Güdemann,
who, after long hesitation, had finally come out against
the Zionist concept in a pamphlet entiled *National Judaism*. Nordau's appearance in *Die Welt* had a powerful
effect. That Güdemann had suffered a defeat was purely
secondary. The sensational fact—and one which buoyed
the spirits of all Zionists—was that a man of Nordau's
stature had openly espoused the Jewish-state idea.

The importance of Nordau's act was heightened by a
particular circumstance which may be difficult for the
modern reader to believe: At the time all this was happening, a man who favored the establishment of a Jewish

state and considered it feasible was regarded by many
people as quite simple crazy. Nor do I mean "crazy in the
sense the word is applied to an eccentric, to a "queer
bird," but in the normal medical sense: mentally ill,
insane.

Herzl himself was a victim of this prevalent attitude.
At the very start, when he told his friends in Paris that he
intended to work for the creation of a Jewish state, he
knew from their shocked looks and from certain unmistakable remarks that they thought he had lost his mind. One
woman friend burst into tears when she heard that Theodor Herzl had a Jewish state "on the brain."

Under the psychological pressure of his well-meaning
friends in Paris, Herzl at times came close to doubting his
own sanity. It took all his strength of mind to stand up
under the suspicious or pitying looks and not succumb to
the power of suggestion. He believed in himself and in the
rationality of his idea despite all the tears and admoni-
tions. And he pursued his course.

In Vienna, too, after he had moved there to assume a
top editorial post on the *Neue Freie Presse,* he caught the
same looks and hints: "A very gifted man, indeed a man
of genius, but unfortunately something is not quite right—
you know, the business with the 'Jewish state'...."

Then, all at once, Max Nordau made his appearance in
Die Welt. The astonishment would not have been as great
if he had been merely a well-known writer. But Nordau
was noted for his alertness to anything which departed from
normal standards of mental health. A doctor of medicine
among his other attainments, he had in fact made a spe-
cialty of detecting aberrations in the people and the social
trends of that time. And here was this same Nordau—
the merciless critic, the experienced psychologist, the

author of *The Conventional Lies of Civilized Man* and
other widely read books—proclaiming almost defiantly his
adherence to the Jewish state. The article in *Die Welt*,
with which he moved into the front ranks of the movement, was in effect a medical certificate attesting that the
Zionists were sound of mind and were not pursuing a
hopeless phantom.

Herzl greatly valued Nordau's adherence to the Jewish-
state idea and was gratified at winning such an ally. I
cannot cite any specific words of his to prove this, but I
recall his making frequent remarks on the subject. Not
only did he recognize that the name "Max Nordau" would
lend new prestige to the Zionist cause; he also felt
strengthened by the knowledge that he had in Nordau an
active and valuable collaborator.

One minor detail from this period is interesting for
what it reveals about Herzl. Before me is the original
manuscript of Nordau's article attacking Rabbi Güdemann; it contains some revisions in Herzl's handwriting.

Nordau was not in the habit of handling opponents with
kid gloves. In the first line of his article, he dignified his
victim with the latter's full title, "the Chief Rabbi of
Vienna, Herr Dr. M. Güdemann," and at the very end
he referred to "the Chief Rabbi, Dr. M. Güdemann." But
with that the amenities were at an end. Throughout the
rest of the article, Nordau wrote simply "Herr Güdemann."

To Herzl, however, "Herr Güdemann" sounded too
abrupt. The elderly gentleman—he was then 62—with the
white prophet's beard, who had shown in the past his
personal sympathy for Herzl, was surely entitled to a more
respectful form of address. So Herzl took his pencil and
in each instance placed a "Dr." after the "Herr." It was

only two letters, but it represented a small plaster for the wounds which Nordau had inflicted.

Nordau had signed his name simply "Max Nordau." But here, too, Herzl prefixed a "Dr."—obviously on the assumption that adding the title would lend the article greater authority in the eyes of its readers.

Herzl would have shrunk from making any more extensive changes in the manuscript. He had always been profoundly aware of Nordau's greatness, literary and otherwise, and he paid him the tribute of leaving his manuscripts intact insofar as possible. For that matter, any major edtitorial changes would surely have brought a protest from the author—and Nordau could protest vigorously indeed when the occasion required.

But, above all, Herzl never forgot that his friend Nordau had stood by him during those dark days in Paris when most others saw in the Jewish-state idea only the product of a sick mind.

15

BESIDES HERZL AND MYSELF, *Die Welt* had a third editor, Dr. Saul Rafael Landau. A lawyer by profession and about 30 years of age, he was well-built and approximately Herzl's height. He was goodlooking, with a short, brown goatee.

At the very bottom of the last page of the magazine were the words: "Publisher: Paul Naschauer. Executive Editor: Dr. S. R. Landau." There was nothing whatever to indicate that the moving spirit of the entire undertaking was actually Herzl.

Landau's editorial role at *Die Welt* was not an impressive one. He devoted very little time to the day-by-day chores of putting out the magazine, and his visits to the printshop or our *Rembrandtstrasse* office were rare events. I never once saw him in Herzl's study, where most of our work was done. He contributed occasional articles and short items, but, in general, his absence from the editorial board would not have made the slightest difference.

Paul Naschauer, who was listed as publisher, was Herzl's brother-in-law. A pleasant, middle-aged man, he was slim, blond, of medium height, and a stylish dresser. His relations with Herzl were warm, and it was apparent that he freely acknowledged the latter's superiority as something which did honor to all those linked to him by blood or marriage.

It was my understanding that Naschauer was then a leading figure at the Vienna fruit and produce exchange and a very wealthy man. He undoubtedy played some part in supporting *Die Welt*.

He visited our *Rembrandtstrasse* office quite often and was always unaffectedly cordial, with none of the airs of a "publisher." He was interested in the magazine's affairs, but never interfered in editorial or administrative matters.

Naschauer was much better educated and more widely read than the average businessman. Once, at our office, he made a chance reference to the so-called "basic-laws" which provided the juridical foundation of certain states. Dr. Landau, who happened to be present, promptly asked in an offensively pedagogical manner: "Do you know our basic law? Do you know what it is?" Whereupon Nas-

chauer good-humoredly proceeded to quote the verbatim
text of the statute like a well-prepared law student in the
examination hall.

*   *   *

On June 17, when I arrived at Herzl's house as usual,
he asked me: "Have you read yesterday's *Ostdeutche
Rundschau?*" He asked the question very matter-of-factly,
as he rummaged among some papers on his desk. I replied
that I hadn't. "Read it," he said, still quite imperturbable.
"You will find in it the first lead article that it has ever
been your lot to inspire." That was all, and the subject
was never referred to again.

Full of curiosity as to what I might have to do with the
lead article, I obtained a copy of the *Rundschau,* a Viennese paper, during the course of the day. My questions
were quickly answered. The article dealt with a short
item I had written for the "Week" column in the second
issue of *Die Welt.* In it, I had criticized the excessive preoccupation of Austria's German and Czech-speaking Jews
with trifling issues of domestic politics, which caused them
to neglect the most vital Jewish problems. I closed with
the words: "Of course, the Jews have no other troubles.
Of what importance is the ghetto which is rising like a
threatening cloud on the Austrian horizon! Of what importance is the misery of our Galician, Rumanian and
Russian brothers, who are rotting in poverty!"

My remarks had outraged the anti-Semitic *Ostdeutche
Rundschau.* However, its attack was directed less at *Die
Welt* than at the great Viennese daily, the *Neue Freie
Presse.* Herzl was, of course, not only editor-in-chief of the
Zionist *Welt* but also a member of the *Presse's* editorial
staff. The *Rundschau* was exploiting this fact to discredit

the *Presse* by making it responsible for statements and opinions which appeared in *Die Welt*. My brief item was actually only a pretext, for other Viennese papers had previously used the same tactics against the *Presse*.

Herzl had been aware from the start that the item in question might have repercussions. When I originally showed it to him, he had read it carefully and then hesitated. "That's a dangerous item."

"It represents our viewpoint," I replied.

He hesitated again and then suddenly, as though brushing aside his misgivings, threw it on the pile of manuscripts destined for the printer.

The outcome must have been most painful to Herzl. Yet, he never showed the slightest trace of anger or irritation afterward. It was as though he accepted such episodes with philosophical resignation and, moreover, had said to himself: I read the item, accepted it, printed it—the responsibility is mine.

A quarter of a century later, when Herzl's *Diaries* were published, I learned that the *Ostdeutche Rundschau's* article had led to an exchange of words with Moriz Benedikt, one of the publishers of the *Neue Freie Presse*. Benedikt had declared: "*Die Welt* is a source of great embarrassment to us. It would be better if it ceased publication." To which Herzl had replied: "That is out of the question."

* * *

I do not see how anyone who had once looked into Herzl's brown eyes could ever forget them. Roundish rather than oval, they were framed by finely formed lids and somewhat deep-set. When one spoke with Herzl, it was his eyes above all that fixed one's attention. Not that he made any deliberate attempt to "hypnotize" his listeners; in his daily relations with other people, he was perfectly natural and unaffected. Rather, if one sometimes glimpsed a radiance in his eye which was out of the ordinary, it was a reflection of his personality, which was surely out of the ordinary.

The magnetic quality of his eyes stemmed from the spiritual life which could be read so clearly in them. Again and again, the thought occurred to one: The noblest East speaks out of these eyes. Which Biblical prophet, which ancient prince may it have been who bore these same lineaments? After innumerable generations, the very image of a man long vanished springs suddenly from the bosom of a nation, and flames which blazed millennia ago glow once again in the eye of a descendant.

Herzl's eyes were highly expressive. Above all, they were earnest and alert; they seemed to observe and comprehend everything, to peer into the secret places of men's souls. Who can say how many people may have come to Herzl with some dishonest intention, only to abandon their schemes after confronting those eyes which penetrated all masks and all deception?

Each of Herzl's moods found its appropriate and engaging expression in his eyes. He was never given to exaggerated facial contortions. Only once did I ever see him grimace: In order to make his three children laugh for a photograph, he made a funny face. His eyes could be solemn, they could be gay and rougish, they could flash with righteous anger, and they could be tender when he caressed one of his children.

He had a curious way of looking at a friend as he shook hands to take leave. He would lower his head slightly, rolling his eyes with a wordlessly elequent expression, as though exchanging a silent pledge.

16

WITH THE SUMMER HEAT approaching, Herzl announced one day: "We're leaving for the country soon." His wife and children, it appeared would go to Bad Ischl together with his parnets; while he himself would stay in Reichenau for some time. He added that he hoped the editorial routine of the *Die Welt* would proceed without a hitch during his absence.

It was not welcome news; the thought that Herzl might leave Vienna had not even occurred to me. However, I felt by now sufficiently familiar with my editorial duties to carry on with a measure of autonomy. I had also learned enough about Herzl's ideas and wishes so that I had no fear of taking some action that would be grossly at variance with his thinking.

Of course, *Die Welt* had another editor, Dr. Landau, but he was more or less automatically left out of consideration. Herzl had more confidence in me than in him, and, for my part, I had the feeling that in any emergency I could count on myself better than on him. As far as Landau himself was concerned, he was only too willing to agree to an arrangement which lifted the responsibility from his shoulders and left him more time for other pursuits.

In any event, I was comforted by the thought that Reichenau was only an hour and a half from Vienna by train, so that it would not be difficult to contact Herzl in case of need.

The Upper Austrian spa Bad Ischl, where Herzl's family were to spend their holiday, was known for attracting a large number of Jewish guests from Austria-Hungary and other countries; Viennese Jews were particularly well represented. Ischl was popular less for the curative powers of its salt and sulphur springs than for its salubrious climate and for the pleasure of being among friends.

As soon as Herzl's family had left for Ischl, *Die Welt's* editorial offices were moved from his home to the official headquarters at No. 11 *Rembrandtstrasse.*

Herzl's family was going away for a holiday, but *he* had no intention of abandoning himself to sweet idleness in the country. "A great deal of work awaits me at Reichenau," he said to me. "Preparations for the congress. Completing the welcoming speech. Assigning the reports. And letters, letters. . . ."

It was a sacrifice for Herzl to separate himself from his family. Had his mind not been so filled with plans for the congress and other Zionist matters, he would never have spent the vacation weeks given him by the *Neue Freie Presse* away from those dear to him. His colleagues on the *Presse* used the time to loaf a bit and rest their weary brains after the year's exertions. But Herzl felt he could not permit himself anything like that. Several times, speaking of the Zionist movement, he had said to me: "If I should stop working today, the whole apparatus would come to a standstill." And what he said was true. He had invented the apparatus, he had constructed it, and now he serviced it—a master mechanic whom no one could replace. Who knows what might have happened if at that stage in the development of Zionism he had turned away from it.

Herzl had a very cogent reason for spending these weeks of concentrated work in Reichenau rather than Vienna: He wanted to put ample distance between himself and the

Neue Freie Presse. Had he remained in the city, he would have run the constant risk, even though he was on vacation, of being suddenly pressed into service by one of the editors to write some absolutely vital, frightfully urgent article. For there is no one quite so ruthless as a newspaper editor in quest of a story.

In Reichenau, Herzl hoped to devote himself undisturbed to his Zionist work. Open and concealed foes of the congress, who would gladly have strangled it in the cradle, were already stirring in Jewish circles, and defensive measures were necessary. Once, at the *Rembrandtstrasse,* Herzl said to me: "God protect the congress against the Jews; there will be no need to protect it against the anti-Semites."

There existed a "preparatory commission" for the congress, but, like most of the commissions and committees which had sprung up around Herzl, it was more decorative than effective. It was essentially out of modesty that Herzl permitted the formation of these bodies; though he had himself created everything of real importance, he was perfectly willing to see some of the reflected glory of his own achievements fall upon his associates.

Occasionally, there were little palace revolutions, with the preparatory commission protesting against Herzl's allegedly autocratic and arbitrary behavior. Then he would have to calm the teapot tempest by giving the rebels new assurances of the vital role they would play in the success of the undertaking.

Far more serious than these petty uprisings, however, was the increasing opposition to Herzl's Zionist activities which was developing in the executive offices of the *Neue Freie Presse.* What was involved here was his very material existence and the welfare of his family. He was having sharper and sharper exchanges with his employers, who demanded that he sever his connections with *Die Welt* and the Zionist movement. From day to day, he expected the final break, which would mean either resignation or dismissal.

If this happened, Herzl would lose more than just his livelihood. He would also forfeit a journalistic and literary position which it had taken years of hard work to achieve, a top-ranking editorial post which was at once a position of power and a pinnacle of literary eminence. It was a truly agonizing inner conflict. For which should he decide: *Die Welt* or the great Viennese daily? Among intimate friends, Herzl spoke frankly of this painful dilemma, with the result that the whole affair inevitably became common knowledge.

Through the indiscretion of a young relative of Herzl's wife, I had learned roughly what his financial situation was; it was a comfortable one. Nevertheless, it was obvious that, if he lost his position with the *Neue Freie Presse,* he would scarcely be able to maintain his family's previous scale of living, even though this had been well within the bounds of moderation.

And yet it should not be thought that Herzl was visibly tottering under the weight of his inner struggle. He bore his troubles fatalistically, prepared for both a favorable and an unfavorable outcome. Basically an optimist by temperament, he had the capacity to drive worries from his head at least temporarily when the situation required it.

17

ONE SUNDAY MORNING, I was drowsing on my sofa, wondering whether on not to go out, when there was a knock at the door. Probably one of my friends. . . . Half sitting up, I called out: "Come in!" The moment I saw who my visitor was, I jumped from my sofa in delighted surprise. It was Herzl.

I greeted him respectfully and asked him to be seated, wondering what urgent business might have brought him to my room. But he merely asked casually, as though he had been one of my student comrades: "Rosenberger, would you like to stroll about with me for a while?" I said I would be only too happy to, and in a moment we were off.

In the early period of his Zionist activity, Herzl did not husband his time as jealously as in later days. He was not yet troubled by the thought that a man's life was a fleeting thing and that each hour, indeed each second, must be utilized for the cause as something precious that would never return. He was anything but a carefree time-waster when I came to know him in the spring of 1897, but he was not yet a slave of the clock. He was willing to take a few hours off when, as on that Sunday morning, he felt a need for relaxation.

We walked at a leisurely pace, chatting casually about the Zionist movement as well as other matters. Nothing of an "official" nature came up; it was simply a pleasant stroll. Once, Herzl pointed to a passing streetcar, with its conductor standing outside on a small platform. "Has it ever occurred to you, he asked, "that a streetcar conductor spends half his life on a little stand that scarcely has room for his feet?" He was in a good humor. Like a true reporter he took notice of everything happening about him and automatically provided some commentary.

Strolling aimlessly, we came to the University. An elderly beggar was standing nearby. Herzl gave him a coin; then, after walking on a short distance, he stopped and, taking his watch from out of his vest pocket said: "Let's wait a minute and make a check on how many passersby pay him any attention." The street was fairly deserted, so that, during our brief check period, the old man enjoyed very few of the blessings of the "golden Vienna heart." Shaking his head slightly, Herzl put his watch back in his pocket. "In the Jewish state," he remarked, "there will be no beggars standing in front of our university."

As we passed the Arcade Café on the *Universitätstrasse,* I observed in a low voice: "Fritz Austerlitz is sitting over there." Herzl glanced at the seats in the colonnade. Austerlitz had surely recognized him, but no greeting was exchanged.

Freidrich Austerlitz, a first-rate journalist, was together with Victor Adler the decisive influence on the Viennese Social Democratic paper, *Arbeiter-Zeitung.* Both had abandoned Judaism, and they dismissed the scheme for founding a Jewish state as an aberration of overimaginative utopian minds. Their anti-Zionism also had a practical side. At that time, there was as yet no well-developed Social Democratic Jewish workers' movement, and the *Arbeiter-Zeitung* had reason to fear that a Jew who embraced Zionism was lost to the Social Democratic party. In Vienna and throughout Austria, there were numerous Jewish workers and commercial employes; the Jewish proletariat in Galicia numbered many thousands and was sunk in poverty. Needless to say, the Social Democrats wished these multitdues to put their faith in Karl Marx rather than Theodor Herzl. Another source of conflict was the fact that the Social Democratic movement was "internationalist" while the Zionist movement was "Jewish nationalist." The gulf seemed unbridgeable, and the two groups remained vigorously opposed to each other.

"Austerlitz writes a great many of the *Arbeiter-Zeitung's* editorials," I remarked.

Herzl did not reply. I had a suspicion that he had read very little of Austerlitz's work, perhaps none of it. He was sublimely ignorant of everything in the way of Viennese journalism that did not emanate from the *Neue Freie Presse's* offices at at No. 11 *Fichtegasse*. His viewpoint was very simple: Whatever was worth knowing appeared in the *Presse,* and what did not appear in the *Presse* was not worth knowing, or at least not essential. Hence, it was a waste of energy to scrutinize all the lesser Viennese papers day after day.

As we walked along noting various people and places, I could not help wondering whether Herzl planned to turn our Sunday-morning stoll into a *feuilleton.* If so, he offered no hint of his intention. Indeed, he made it a practice never to advertise his literary projects in advance. In this he differed from other writers of my acquaintance who loudly announced their forthcoming productions and then, often as not, failed to produce.

A short distance beyond Trinity Church, we encountered two pretty girls of about 17 or 18. As we passed, one of them said rather loudly with youthful unconstraint: "That's Herzl."

The subject of her remark did not so much as change expression. Then, after we had gone a few more steps, he said matter-of-factly: "If I were still young, I'd turn around and go after them." ((He was then 37—no longer young!)

How Herzl had been when he was half that young (or old) I did not, of course, know. At the time I knew him, however, he was anything but the type of man who loses his head at the sight of a petticoat and is ready to rush into a romantic adventure. His attractive appearance and many winning qualities would have made feminine conquests an easy matter. But, quite apart from the fact that he was a married man and a father (not necessarily an iron-clad guarantee of virtue), the leader of the Zionist movement directed his thoughts and efforts to other goals.

At another point in our walk, Herzl remarked: "I'm omitting everying in Kürschner except *The Jewish State* and *The Palais Bourbon.*" "Kürschner" referred to *Kürschner's Calandera of German Literature,* a Who's Who of German-language authors, poets, journalists and editors, from the most celebrated to the most obscure, which provided biographical information and a list of published works, if any. *The Palais Bourbon* was a collection of brilliant essays from Herzl's Paris days. It was interesting that he considered the *Bourbon* and *The Jewish State* the only two of his works which were worth listing after his name.

At noon, the two Sunday strollers bent their steps, at Herzl's suggestion, to a restaurant in the *Josefstadt* district of Vienna.

18

ON JUNE 24, HERZL BEGAN HIS summer vacation. I had assumed he would go directly to Reichenau and was therefore surprised when he told me he would first visit his family in Ischl. I knew that the situation at the *Neue Freie Presse* had reached a critical point. Would he at last be forced to yield to his employer's pressure and, with a heavy heart, abandon his beloved *Welt*? It seemed obvious that he was now going to Ischl to discuss just this problem with his father, whose experience, wisdom and practical good sense he highly respected.

At this point, I was greatly encouraged by receiving a postcard which Herzl had sent just before his departure for Ischl. It read:

"Dear Rosenberger,

"Please don't forget to send me at Ischl, as soon as possible, the Father Ignatius article which Hechler dictated to you (in translation) .

Best regards,

HERZL

6/24/97
Railroad station, Vienna"

This hardly seemed like the sort of card Herzl would have written if he had been preparing to bid *Die Welt* farewell. Even at the railroad station, where he must have had many other things to occupy his mind, his thoughts had been dominated by the magazine.

The Father Ignatius to whom Herzl referred was an English monk who lived in St. Anthony's Abbey in Wales.

His article for *Die Welt* was suffused with love for the Jewish people and for Zion. In it, he said:

"The Jews *must* once again have a definite home on earth, a country, a constitution, an assured center to which those of them that are homeless and cast out can direct their steps, where they can lay their heads to rest in honor."

And further:

"The Jews have already made divine truth known to all the peoples of the earth. The name Zion has become a blessing and an inspiration for untold myriads. In St. Paul's Cathedral in London, in St. Peter's Church in Rome, in St. Peter's Cathedral in Vienna, in St. Isaac's Church in Moscow, in the Cathedral of Notre Dame in Paris, it is impossibe to hold a divine service into whose ritual the literature of Jerusalem, the songs of Zion have not been woven. The Jews are God's chosen instrument; they have, as their prophets foretold, performed many wonders among the peoples of the earth, and in the future they shall also carry out the other prophecies."

. At the bottom of the article, Father Ignatius wrote: "In love for Zion, I sign *Ignatius*."

While Herz was absent from Vienna, I endlessly asked myself the same question: What will his decision be? I tried not to think of what it would mean if the worst came to pass and he broke away from the Zionist movement. And then one day, perhaps five days after his departure, I was sitting at my desk at No. 11 Rembrandtstrasse, buried in manuscripts and galley proofs, when the door opened and I looked into two familiar, smiling eyes: It was Herzl.

I was overjoyed to see him again. We discussed matters pertaining to the magazine, and I showed him the latest mail and other papers. From his undiminished interest

—to me, it seemed, if anything, heightened—I readily concluded which way the die had been cast. He looked better than when I had last seen him and was in good spirits. The country air, the change of scenery and the visit with his family had obviously been beneficial.

Herzl explained that he was stopping in Vienna only briefly before leaving for Reichenau to continue preparations for the congress. He had made his decision: He would remain faithful to the Jewish state and *Die Welt;* as far as the *Neue Freie Presse* was concerned, he would simply take his chances.

" I would like you to come out to Reichenau on Sunday," he said. "There will be work to do for *Die Welt.*"

He gave me the train schedule and said he would be staying at the Hotel Thalhof. Then he dictated a number of letters, most of them pertaining to the congress.

Sunday morning, I took the train to Reichenau. When I entered Herzl's hotel room, he was seated at a table by the open window, pen in hand. On the table were a bottle of ink and various papers. The window looked out on a small garden.

"Quid novi ex Vindobona?"

I replied that there was nothing much new in Vienna.

How did Reichenau and the surrounding region strike me?

"Delightful!" Then, looking out at the garden, I remarked: "It must be . . ."

". . . pleasant working here?" Herzl completed the sentence. And he shook his head and said: "The work is not going very well." He did not look as well as he had in Vienna a few days before.

As I was unpacking the papers I had brought with me, he said: "No, first stroll around a bit. Be back by noon. And save your appetite; you're going to have a good meal."

I didn't wander far from the hotel. Under other circumstances, I would have taken more interest in the mountains, trees and meadows all around, but at that moment I was thinking chiefly of the man inside at the writing-table. It distressed me to see him looking poorly. It was obviously overexertion. He was taking too much of a burden upon himself.

After a short while, I returned to the hotel and told Herzl that I had had my fill of walking. "Good," he said, "then let's begin." He dictated several letters, and, while I transcribed them for his signature, he looked through the material for *Die Welt* which I had brought along. It occurred to me that the room might not be the most favorable for working, for the voices of a woman and two children—hotel guests—came through the open window from the garden outside.

After lunch, we discussed the articles and shorter items that were to appear in the next issue. Then Herzl dictated a few more letters to prospective congress delegates.

In the room there was a full-length mirror, and, as Herzl paced the floor giving dictation, his glance occasionally fell upon his image in the glass. He had every reason to take pleasure in what he saw, and yet one might have supposed from his behavior that he was looking at the likeness of a stranger. I never saw the slightest indication that Herzl was vain about his appearance. He must have known that he was a handsome man, but he never gave an outward sign of that knowledge.

Late in the afternoon, as the time approached for my departure, I gathered together the manuscripts which we had made ready for the printer. Herzl accompanied me to the station. As we walked slowly through the country-side, which united all the varied charms of mountain and valley, he held forth on the features of the landscape: the Rax, the Schneeberg, the Schwarzach Valley, the Rax Plateau. He told me about the owners of the Hotel Thal-hof and mentioned in passing that the hotel was some 500 meters above sea level. He didn't lecture or declaim; he merely reported in his normal conversational tone. If I had taken it all down in my notebook, the result would have been a delightful Herzl *feuilleton*.

19

TYPOGRAPHICAL ERRORS ARE one of the occupational hazards of the jouralistic profession. The blame for a "typo" falls on three persons: the typesetter who made the original error, the proof-reader at the print-shop, and the editor, whose job it is to see that the "galleys" are read. If the editor naively assumes that the printer's proof-reader is infallible, the "typo" gremlin is apt to have a field day.

On July 9, five days after my trip to Reichenau, I received the following letter:

"*Thalhof, July 8, 1897*

"*Dear Rosenberger,*

"There is a most unpleasant typographical error in 'The Week': '*angespuckt*' ['spat at'] instead of '*angeulkt*' ['jeered at']. It reminds one of the lies that appear in certain papers whose tone I despise, and it may result in an official correction.

"I have agreed to Knopf's proposal to move the mailing department to the *Rembrandtstrasse*.

"Please bring me 50 *Welt* letterhead sheets and envelopes when you come out. This time, I wish you would come on *Saturday*, taking the 1:15 p.m. train from Vienna. Please bring along the morning mail from the *Rembrandtstrasse*. Have Kollinski mail me what comes later. I would like you to spend the night here and remain until Sunday evening.

Best regards,

Th. H."

The typographical error appeared in the "Week" column on page 3 of the sixth issue of *Die Welt*. Before me is the manuscript, written in pencil in Herzl's characteristic hand, and there on the third page, clear and legible, is the ill-fated word: *"angeulkt."*

Just who had been *"angeulkt"* or ridiculed, according to this account by Herzl? None other than His Honor, the Mayor of Vienna, Dr. Carl Leuger. The anti-Semitic ringleader Dr. Lueger had made a propaganda junket to the Austrian-Hungarian frontier in order to stir up the Christian population against their Jewish compatriots. In the city of Pressburg, he and his entourage had wandered by error into a street inhabited largely by Jews. There he was recognized and greeted with loud shouts of "Away with Leuger!" and sundry other gibes. The police moved in at once, but did they take action against the itinerant agitator Dr. Lueger? Not at all. They arrested several Jews for "creating a disturbance."

The word *"Ulk"* ("joke"), from which *"angeulkt"* is derived, is more common in Germany than in Austria and may have been unfamiliar to the Viennese typesetter.

Those of a psychoanalytical turn of mind may go further and attribute the error to a 'Freudian slip." For the typesetter was a Social Democrat, and the Viennese Social Democrats of those days were anything but kindly disposed toward Dr. Leuger and his Christian Social party.

In any event, the "typo" had no repercussions. The official correction by Leuger, which Herzl feared, failed to materialize.

*   *   *

On Tuesday, July 6, the group of Zionist doctors headed by J. Schalit had returned to Vienna after tendnig wounded soldiers from the Greek-Turkish War in Turkish military hospitals. I met Schalit on the 9th and suggested that he also go to Reichenau. He did so two days later and reported to Herzl on the experiences of the Jewish medical expedition.

That Sunday evening, after receiving some last instructions from Herzl preparatory to my departure for Vienna, I took my papers from the desk and remarked: "Now that Schalit is back, of course, my term of office at *Die Welt* has expired." I said it as matter-of-factly as I could, as though referring to an accomplished fact which I had no intention of trying to change.

I explained: "It was decided that I would fill in for Schalit while he was away."

Now Herzl realized that I was speaking of resigning His reply was short and to the point. He put his hand on my shoulder and said: "You're staying!"

When I was about to object, he repeated firmly, almost as though giving an order: "You're staying!" Then, quickly changing the subject, he reviewed his instructions for the next issue of the magazine.

Among the manuscripts which I brought to Reichenau to show Herzl was one whose history may bear mentioning. A few days earlier, as I was making my usual inspection of the newspapers at the Café Central, my eye had been caught by a strange item in the *Berliner Tageblatt*. It was a solemn manifesto of the "Rabbinical Association of Germany," signed by five Rabbis of Berlin, Frankfurt, Breslau, Halberstadt and Munich. The document opened as follows:

"The endeavors of so-called Zionists to found a Jewish national state in Palestine are contrary to the messianic promises of Judaism as contained in Holy Scripture and later religious sources."

The concluding sentence was:

"Religion and patriotism alike therefore impose upon us the duty of urging all those who have the welfare of Judaism at heart to shun the aforementioned Zionist endeavors and, in particular, the congress which, despite all warnings, is still being planned."

I read this declaration at the Café Central, was overcome by righteous indignation, and promptly wrote a furious article. I presented the rabbis' statement at the beginning —placed it, as it were, in the pillory—and then proceeded to analyze it, endowing the five authors with the title of "the protest-rabbis."

Upon arriving in Reichenau, I submitted my article to Herzl. He read the rabbis' lament, then my wrathful commentary, and marked several passages in the margin as though to express agreement. When he nodded approvingly at the end, my last doubts were laid to rest: The article was accepted and would appear, and the honorable protest-rabbis would get their comeuppance.

But it was not to be. Herzl paid me compliments and praised my "polemical talents" . . . but the article was too sharp. "I will myself assume the task of conveying our opinion to the five gentlemen," he said, and added smilingly: "With your permission, I will borrow your word 'protest-rabbi' from the article for the general behoof." The result was that issue no. 7 of *Die Welt* (July 16, 1897) contained a lead article by Herzl entitled "Protest-rabbis." It was, of course, far superior to mine in both literary style and moderation of tone; at the same time, it brilliantly settled accounts with the five protesters and deflated their accusations.

The term "protest-rabbi" became a permanent part of our *Welt* vocabulary and was used to categorize a certain type of anti-Zionist. It did considerable damage to its original targets and their supporters, for other rabbis were anxious to avoid being lumped together with the "protest-rabbis." I thus had the satisfaction—albeit anonymously— of seeing my coinage render good service to the cause.

Issue no. 7 of *Die Welt,* which contained Herzl's article, enjoyed a further distinction: It was confiscated by the Public Presecutor's office in Vienna. However, this minor calamity had nothing to do with the Case of the Five Rabbis, as the next chapter will show.

20

*D*IE WELT HAD AROUSED THE Public Prosecutor's displeasure by accurately reporting an anti-Semitic outbreak which had occurred in the town of Tarnow in Galicia. The outrages, which followed a tavern brawl, were committed by soldiers of the 57 Infantry Regiment stationed in Tarnow. *Die Welt* quoted an account in the Polish-language Cracow daily *Dziennik Krakówski*, as follows:

". . . Friday evening, [the soldiers] attacked citizen Weinfeld and injured him severely in the head. Saturday morning, they also injured several Jews. On Sunday, a veritable state of siege prevailed. All doors had to be barred. The soldiers marched through the streets with drawn bayonets, beating and stabbing any Jew who crossed their path. The police drove the people off the streets but did not interfere with the soldiers in their 'work.' Despite the sending of a deputation to the district administrator and the military commandant, no security measures were taken. Many people have already been injured, including a 14-year-old girl. [Police] patrols march past the rioting soldiers without disturbing them. I saw a corporal of the 57th Infantry Regiment wreck a poor Jew's shop while the police patrol cursed at the Jews for not going home."

The Public Prosecutor's office found the whole affair most painful. Not because anti-Semitic rioting had occurred—there was nothing unusual in that—but because the rioters were soldiers of the Imperial Army whose duty was supposedly to preserve law and order and insure the safety of all citizens. Not only that, but the local authorities, who should have put an end to the outrage, had stood by and done nothing.

How should the matter be dealt with? Obviously, what had been done could not be undone. Hence, there was nothing left but to resort to an old and tested remedy: The paper that reported the embarrassing occurrences was confiscated. No point in letting people at home and abroad know what had been happening up in Galicia.

Herzl took the confiscation calmly. He was prepared for episodes of that sort, which in no way shook his determination to employ free expression of opinion on behalf of his oppressed co-religionists. Moreover, we enjoyed a stroke of good fortune: Official red tàpe delayed the confiscation until the day after the issue had been mailed out, with the result that all our regular subscribers received their copies. The usual confiscation ceremonies then proceeded. Uniformed policemen marched placidly from coffeehouse to coffeehouse and from news-vendor to news-vendor, collecting all copies of *Die Welt*. The café habitués generally took no notice whatever of this familiar ritual.

One point should be made in connection with the events at Tarnow. However reprehensible, they were very different from the periodic pogroms suffered by the Jews in Tsarist Russia. The pogroms, as a rule, were officially or at least semi-officially inspired. They had a deliberate function—that of using the Jews as a lightning-rod to draw off popular discontent—and they generally ended in large-scale bloodshed and other crimes. By comparison, the misdeeds of the soldiers at Tarnow were fairly mild. Jews were "merely" beaten and stabbed, not murdered, and the outbreak was wholly spontaneous, with no official provocation. In fact, the local military and civil authorities were undoubtedly given a stiff reprimand by Vienna afterward and warned to do their duty if another such incident ever occurred.

It was not difficult for the rioting soldiers in Tarnow to identify the Jews among the town population, for their special dress, side-curls, etc. made them readily recognizable. Indeed, I recall a story in this connection which has the double virtue of being historically true and of being available in Herzl's words. Thus, we read in an article by Herzl in issue no. 6 of *Die Welt*:

"The Hungarian writer Agai tells in a *feuilleton* the following pretty story. Once he was in Ostend together with a Hungarian bishop, who was wearing boots under his long coat. A long coat and boots, however, are the identifying marks by which the Ostend street urchins recognize Polish Jews. Hence, they ran along behind the bishop, taunting him and pelting him with stones, as they make a practice of doing to Polish Jews who come to Ostend. The clerical gentleman was utterly beside himself and looked for a policeman to protect him from the boys' inexplicably mischievous behavior. When he asked the policeman what was the matter with them, the officer smiled good-naturedly: 'Oh, they act that way with Jews.' 'What do you mean, Jew? I am a bishop!' And he threw back his coat so that the astounded policeman could see the large golden cross. However, when the bishop, much agitated as a result of his adventure, rejoined his fellow-countryman Agai and told him what had happened, the latter said: 'Now you see, Your Grace, what it is like to be a Jew. You tasted it for only a quarter of an hour; we have endured it for 1,800 years. . . .'"

As we have already seen, Herzl took the confiscation of an issue of *Die Welt* with complete equanimity. However, the incident which precipitated it, and the fate of the Tarnow Jews, left him anything but unmoved. His mood, one of bitter resignation, was expressed in a brief commentary that appeared in the "Week" column of *Die Welt*:

"An anti-Semitic outrage in Tarnow. We record it like the others that come to us from all over the world. There will be many more like it. We record the doleful event without attempting to exaggerate; it is no more significant than the others, and, unfortunately, no more insignificant. This time, it was soldiers who committed outrages against the Jews. . . .Things were exactly the same in the dark ages of history, which we cannot recall without anguish. A bit of the Middle Ages staggers raw and bloody through the streets of a modern city, and there is fear—the old fear that returns again and again. All that is really new is that the report appears in every paper in the world the following day—and is forgotten the day after that. Perhaps that is how it must be. That is as far as public opinion goes in getting aroused about such things. It takes note of the occurrence just as it takes note of the new moon, the first snow or the fist cockchafer. The Jews are obviously there so that outrages can be committed against them from time to time. Perhaps that is their 'mission' for which so many are searching."

21

A FTER STARING PENSIVELY for a time at some papers on his desk, Herzl suddenly looked up and said:

"After all, we don't want our friends to be sent to Siberia."

For a moment, I didn't follow his train of thought; then I replied: "Certainly not. It's a heavy responsibility . . ."

This rather mysterious exchange had to do with the forthcoming Zionist congress, which at that particular moment was the target of hostile maneuvers emanating from the south German city of Munich. Herzl had selected

Munich as the site of the congress. As he expressed it in *Die Welt:* "The charming, hospitable city of Munich was chosen because it is a crossroads of the great new highways of the nations."

The congress was originally to have taken place in Zürich, but there were sound objections to this. The congress delegates included many Russian Jews. In Russian Government circles, however, Zürich enjoyed a very special reputation as a gathering place for revolutionists and conspirators. It was regarded as a city which opened its gates impartially to politicians of every persuasion, including those who bore the rulers of Tsarist Russia no great love. Hence, the ruling circles in St. Petersburg would probably sniff sedition in any Jewish congress held in Zürich, and they might well ship the returning Russian delegates to a penal colony as soon as they crossed the border. Needless to say, Herzl wanted to lead Russian Jewry to Zion, not to Siberia. He alluded rather cautiously in *Die Welt* to his reasons for abandoning the Zürich plan:

Zürich had originally been contemplated as the congress site, and the majority of the commission had defeated the first proposal and instead chosen the hospitable and conveniently situated city of Munich only because Zürich is less popular in Eastern Europe as a meeting place."

Everything seemed to be settled and we were already speaking confidently of the "Munich congress" when unfriendly voices began reaching our ears from Munich. Their general purport was: We need no Zionists here; we don't want to provide a rendezvous for advocates of a Jewish state; keep away from us and find another place for your congress! Anti-Semites, one would naturally assume. And, indeed, it would not have surprised us to hear that anti-Semitic orators were holding forth in Munich

beer-halls and demanding, to the delighted howls of their
followers, that any Zionist congress be thrown bodily out
of the city. In this instance, however, the familiar cry of
"Out with the Jews!" was coming from quite another quarter—from the confidence chamber of the Jewish Religious
Community of Munich. The governing body of the Jewish
Community had decided that Jews who favored a Jewish
state were not wanted in Munich. What is more, it had
lost no time in communicating this decision in black on
white to the preparatory commission of the Zionist congress, *viz.*: " . . . We are therefore compelled to repeat
our request and, in order to preclude any misunderstanding, to *protest formally against the holding of the congress
in Munich.* Respectfully yours, the Governing Body of the
Jewish Religious Community of Munich."

The letter failed to have the crushing effect that its
authors had probably anticipated. Herzl calmly took notice
of the rebuff and then replied in *Die Welt:*

"The preparatory commission had drawn the necessary
conclusions from these statements. The congress will meet
in Basle on August 29. We are firmly confident that its
proceedings will inspire public opinion with sympathy for
our cause."

And he closed on a conciliatory yet ironical note:

"If the gentlemen from Munich should invite the congress to their city later on, after realizing the error they
made about this movement, the conveners will unquestionably give them preference."

Herzl stated quite bluntly in private conversation what
he expressed only guardedly on paper. "They should regard it as an honor if we come to them in Munich," he
said to me, lifting his head proudly and strongly accenting
the first syllable of the word "honor."

Herzl's reply to the Munich Religious Community was signed with the six-pointed Star of David. He sometimes used this or the Shield of David as a signature in place of his name.

The decision to hold the congress in Basle won general approval. As Herzl wrote in *Die Welt:*

"The city of Basle was chosen as the congress site because there is no prejudice against it in Eastern Europe and because transportation to it is convenient for people who attend the congress from various countries. Those who were willing to come to Munich will not have to make much more of a sacrifice in time and money in order to go to Basle."

There was no letter of protest from Basle—neither from the Jewish Religious Community nor from its good rabbi, Dr. Cohn. And so the Swiss city of Basle, on the banks of the Rhine, was chosen to play host to the first session of a parliamentary body whose task was to deliberate on the founding of a Jewish state.

22

IN THOSE YEARS—IN FACT, even before Herzl made his appearance—we students used to argue far into the night about the question: Precisely what are the Jews? A race, a nation, a people, a religion, a brotherhood bound by a common fate and a common enemy? Opinions were divided, and the discussions were often very heated. Those who later flocked to Herzl contended that the Jews were a nation.

Indeed, we were living in an era of nationalism, in which the word "nation" provided the basis for a cult which all too often merged into chauvinism. This was less true of the "Jewish nationalists," however, than of other nationalist groups. The Jewish nationalists—whose shock troops were the students, especially the Viennese—held their nationalism proudly aloft as a shield against anti-Semitic abuse. They pounded on the shield in order to rally those Jews whose faith was weakening, and they regarded their nationalism as a first step leading toward Palestine. But they avoided the exaggerated forms which nationalism assumed, for example, among the Germans.

I still recall many of the exchanges that enlivened our discussions of the nature of Judaism. In the old pre-Herzl days, we had a Jewish students' club in Vienna called "Gamala," whose president I had the high honor to be. Each week, we held a lecture and discussion evening in our clubroom. Among the guests one evening was a young foreign Jew named Marcou Baruch of whom we will hear more later. On this occasion, Baruch took part in a debate which among other things touched on the theme. "Are the Jews a racial group?" One of the participants, a Jew from Germany, insisted that German Jews must be regarded as Germans rather than Jews. Baruch, who spoke excellent German with a French accent, remarked in the course of his reply:

"When one tells a Jew that he is descended from apes, he is perfectly willing to believe it; when one tells him that he is descended from Jews, he shakes his head in disbelief."

In Prague, where I completed my first semester of studies at the German University, I once attended a lecture by a Viennese lawyer who had come to propagandize on behalf of Jewish nationalism. At one point in his speech, he started to say:

"We Jews are a nation if only because we have a common enemy . . ."

Whereupon a member of the audience broke in, in a sepulchral voice:

"If it's all a matter of a common enemy, then the fleas are a nation, too."

Everyone laughed, including the speaker, but the latter took care thereafter not to provide any more targets for the sharp Prague Jewish wit.

"Are the Jews a Race?" was the title of an essay which caused Herzl to predict that I would one day be awarded an Austrian decoration known as the Order of Maria Theresa. The latter, which was founded in the mid-18th century during the reign of Empress Maria Theresa, was a most curious kind of decoration: It was awarded not to obedient, dutiful individuals, but to disobedient ones. When a commander in battle deliberately failed to carry out an order because he felt it was mistaken, he received the Order of Maria Theresa—provided, of course, that his insubordiation was vindicated and helped turn defeat into victory.

In this instance, I had definitely been insubordinate and disobeyed the strict instructions of my editor-in-chief, Herzl. The latter had given me the article with directions to have it set in type at once and featured prominently in the magazine. He seemed to take a special interest in the piece, which was written by a man named Leopold Laufer.

Before sending Laufer's manuscript to the printer, I began to read it . . . and was utterly dismayed. It contained so many naive statements in the realm of ethnology and anthropology that it could not possibly appear as it stood.

I promptly sent a long letter to Herzl at Ischl, informing him of my reasons for holding the article back. I quoted various passages and added my own extended commentary. I felt that my editorial conscience was clear, but I still awaited Herzl's next letter with considerable anxiety. When it arrived, it read as follows:

"Ischl, No. 7 Schulgasse

"My dear Rosenberger,

"1. Your arbitrary acts are surely going to win you the Maria Theresa Cross one of these days. Of course, your responsibility extends only to leaving things out, not to putting them it.

"Your critique of Laufer has also made me ashamed of my ignorance. However, I have already given Laufer my word that the essay will appear, and I must keep my promise at all costs. The only solution is as follows: You have it out with Laufer and ask him to revise his article. Point out the contradictions to him and have him eliminate them. If it is not too difficult, you might eliminate them yourself. Editors have that power. I am also returning your pamphlet-sized rebuttal to Laufer's article.

"2. Please send me at once the proofs of Rülf's article (which is to be called: 'German Rabbis. By Dr. L. Rülf (Memel)').

"3. Please have the office boy buy a copy of Güdemann's *National Judaism* at Löwith's on the *Rothenthurmstrasse,* and have it sent in my name to Herr B. Bander in Tarnow for the Rev. Rabbi Feiwisch Scheier.

"4. Klötzl made a mistake on the inside front cover. The *Cook* announcement is placed above the rules of procedure [for the congress]. It should be *under it.* That must be corrected in the next issue. In the next issue, in other words, *the entire announcement of the Zionist Congress must appear again on the inside front cover.*

"5. Please see General Manager Steiner tomorrow and tell him to have 2,000 reprints made of the program and the rules of procedure (to be charged to the congress commission). The Cook announcement is *not* to appear in these in these reprints. The reprints must be prepared at once and *Monday* morning in the following way (as registered printed matter) . . ."

The letter breaks off at this point, since unfortunately only the first two pages have survived intact. Nevertheless, what has been quoted shows clearly Herzl's keen interest in even the smallest details of putting out the magazine.

Not long afterward, I received another letter:

"Ischl, 7/28/97

"My dear Rosenberger,

"Thank you for carrying out my instructions with such precision.

"I now ask you to direct in good order the Exodus from Mizraim in the *Schleifmühlgasse.* All remaining manuscripts must be sent at once to Schöler at No. 3 *Döblinger Hauptstrasse.* He has no 'long primer' [type], so all the 'long primer' has to be set in 'garamond' there.

"Keep an eye particularly on the layout of Zangwill's novel. Have Schöler set the entire remaining part in gd [garamond] immediately and start Chawa Rubin in gd. Also, will you have the boy bring Schöler a few issues of *Die Welt* so that he can familiarize himself in advance with our type distribution and prepare all the necessary fonts.

"Send a polite reply to the queer duck who wrote the enclosed manuscript, telling him that we print only unpublished material and asking him to submit articles that are of topical interest rather than broadly theoretical.

"Please send me some manuscripts this week, too, without delay. I will be in Vienna next Tuesday.

"With best regards,

Yours sincerely,

HERZL."

"Mizraim," which Herzl mentions in his letter, is the Hebrew name for Egypt; he was referring humorously to our "Exodus" from the *Wiener Mode's* printing plant on the *Schleifmühlgasse*.

As it happened, our changeover to a new printer proceeded far more smoothly than Herzl's return to Vienna from Bad Ischl. The latter is situated on a small river called the Traun. Just as Herzl was preparing for his departure, the normally placid little Traun, swollen by torrential rains, overflowed its banks, swept away the bridges, and disrupted railroad and mail service. On July 31, *Die Welt* received a telegram from Ischl marked "urgent": "Mail Service interrupted send nothing for time being Herzl." Herzl had planned to arrive in Vienna on August 3. Instead I received the following letter delivered by heaven only knows what circuitous route:

Ischl, 8/2/97

"*My dear Rosenberger,*

"Isolated and without material as I am here, I will hardly be able to send off 'The Week' today. Consequently, it devolves upon you, gentlemen, to write the paragraphs for 'The Week' in the spirit whose broad lines I have drawn in previous issues. I ask you in particular to keep our temperamental friends Landau and Schalit on the paths of discretion.

"Rülf's reply to Bloch is to appear in the 'Tribune' section.

"Whatever additional material reaches me today and tomorrow, I will send to Schöler by Special Delivery.

"The contents are to be in this order:

" 'Pre-Zionist Figures'

" 'The Week'

" 'German and Polish Jews'

" 'The Mood in Russia'

" 'The Congress'

"I am sending Schöler today the clipping from the *Ungarische Wochenschrift*, which probably won't make [issue] No. 10 any longer but should be placed in the over-matter as an article (brevier type) if there is no room for it.

"With hurried best regards,

'Sincerely yours,

"TH. HERZL."

I also received another telegram from Ischl:

"Impossible send manuscript make Week cautious temperate first article Pre-Zionists second Birnbaum—Herzl."

Herzl's chief concern was to avoid any indiscretions in "The Week." The latter was one of the magazine's more ticklish features; its comments on the passing scene were often rather acid, sometimes perhaps excessively so. I skirted these shoals by devoting "The Week" to some highly lyrical reflections on the 9th day of the Jewish month of Ab, which is the anniversary of the destruction of Jerusalem and hence a day of mourning for Jews.

"Isolated and without material as I am here," Herzl had written—almost a cry of pain. I wondered what he was doing while he was unable to work on *Die Welt*. Was he merely staring sullenly at the flood waters, bewailing the inclemency of the elements? No, that was not Herzl's way. Instead, he took advantage of his enforced idleness to write a *feuilleton* which wove a charming poetic spell about the days he spent in Ischl. It appeared in the *Neue Freie Presse* under the title, "Holiday Flood."

In a few more days, the flood was over and the Traun, after its brief rampage, was again flowing quietly between its banks. On Thursday, August 5, we received a wire: "We be back tomorrow morning—Herzl."

Since his family was remaining at Ischl for a time, Herzl took up temporary lodgings in a Vienna hotel instead of his house on the *Berggasse*. I had the impression that he found an occasional sojourn in a hotel by no means disagreeable. It created the illusion that one was a tourist, and Herzl had always been fond of traveling. The hotel also served as a hideaway, for Herzl's vacation was not yet over and he had no wish to fall into the clutches of his employers at the *Neue Freie Presse;* his work for *Die Welt* and the forthcoming congress was far more important to him than any assignment they might have.

The hotel where Herzl was staying was the Continental, at No. 7 *Praterstrasse.* "Some day, when a Jewish state exists," he said to me, "it will be able to look back upon the most curious places of origin." And indeed, if one were to affix a memorial tablet to every building where Herzl thought, wrote and worked for his Jewish state, it would be a formidable undertaking.

Herzl and I worked together in his hotel room, just as in his study at home. For stretches of time, nothing would be heard but the scratching of our pens and the occasional turning of a sheet of paper. Then one of us would make some matter-of-fact observation or I would raise a point

for Herzl to decide. In general, he allowed me wide lati-
tude in editing manuscripts; some of these we worked on
together and others separately.

Occasionally he would offer a pointer on some aspect
of our craft. Once, for example, I handed him an item I
had written. He read it, reflected a moment and said:
"Never overestimate the reader's education and power of
comprehension." I took it back and gave it a more "popular" treatment.

During these days, Herzl spent considerable time at our
Rembrandtstrasse office and our new printshop on the
Döblinger Hanptstrasse as well as at the hotel. Whenever
he was about to leave one of these places, he would address
me with the unvarying formula: "Rosenberger, come with
me." Then we would set out by various circuitous routes
which he felt would protect his anonymity. Our way generally took us through the heavily Jewish *Leopoldstadt*
district. A few short years later, a similar *incognito* stroll
through the *Leopoldstadt* would have been impossible;
Herzl would have been met with marks of reverent recog-
nition at every step.

Herzl's pace during these walks was leisurely and un-
hurried. At times, he would stare at the ground, lost in
thought. What was the topic of conversation when he
spoke? No need to ask: the congress and *Die Welt*—the
two bridges he was building to a Jewish state.

The zeal with which Herzl sought to bring this new
political entity into the world is illuminated by a comment
he once made to me. One of my first acts upon launching
my journalistic career was to obtain a black-lacquered
leather case, half-way between a lawyer's brief-case and a
doctor's bag. It never left my side and was always bulging
with manuscripts, newspapers, magazines, letters, etc. On

one occasion, Herzl remarked with amusement: "It looks like a midwife's bag." Then he paused and added more seriously: "After all, in a real sense we *are* midwives."

Despite the malicious attacks of its enemies, the projected Zionist congress was taking on more and more solid form. Herzl's organizing letters went out in all directions, like radiations from a central power source, and each day we received a cascade of letters—not only replies but also messages from new friends offering their services to the cause.

Not all those who were to take part in the congress were unconditional Herzl adherents. Several of them, in fact, planned to appear at Basle as an "opposition party." They were good Jews and the word "Zion" struck a powerful chord in their hearts, but they were not prepared to embrace the idea of a Jewish state quite so quickly. Herzl had no objection to this sort of honest opposition: "Our arguments will convince them and bring them over to our side."

There were others, however, who could not be described as a "loyal" opposition. They were coming to Basel to disrupt the proceedings and perhaps even to wreck the congress. Herzl knew of their plans and was prepared. It was clear that the threat to the congress came not from the outside, from the anti-Semites, but from an "enemy within."

Meanwhile, Herzl's vacation had ended and he no longer had to play a game of hide-and-seek. Every weekday afternoon, between 1 and 2, he walked to the *Neue Freie Presse* office on the *Frichtegasse*. Since he often asked me to come along, I was a witness to his incredible capacity for work. To the overwhelming demands of the congress and *Die Welt* were now added once again his duties at the *Presse*.

Moreover, he was particularly anxious to keep his employers' favor since the time was drawing near when he would have to take several days' leave for the trip to Basle. All in all, he assumed a burden of work that would have taxed three or four men.

Schalit and Landau were to accompany Herzl to the congress, leaving me in Vienna as the lone member of *Die Welt's* editorial staff. However, I was by now sufficiently experienced at my work so that the prospect did not trouble me.

Herzl commented, punning on the name of our magazine: "Now you will be Atlas, with the entire world resting on your shoulders. But I can rely on your carrying power."

23

THE FATEFUL DAYS WERE approaching when the Zionist congress which Herzl had fashioned with so much love and toil would prove either a living reality or a house of cards. The three days of the congress—August 29, 30 and 31—would be memorable and quite possibly decisive for the Zionist movement.

In this atmosphere of expectancy, with a hundred other things to preoccupy him, Herzl might well have been excused for giving little thought to *Die Welt*. And yet, from Ischl where he had gone for a short rest with his family, I received a "hasty" letter—so hasty, in fact, that Herzl had forgotten to sign it:

"Ischl, 8/22/97

"My dear Rosenberger,

"Just a few hasty words.

"The first article is Birnbaum's 'Ideal Help.'

"The *feuilleton* is Salo Deutsch's excellent 'Massacre.'

"Starting tomorrow, send all letters to Basle.

   "Contents:

"1. Dr. N. Birnbaum, 'The Ideal Help.'

"2. 'The Week.'

"3. Lublinski (or Liebhardt—I don't know how he signs it): 'The Congress and the German Jews.'

"4. 'Hungarian Moods,' if no 'New York Letter' arrives. I authorize you to open the letters from America addressed to me and, if there is a usable one, to run it.

"5. The Congress (show the Kokesch items to Werner).

"6. ,etc. *Feuilleton:* 'Massacre," by Salo Deutsch.

"I hope everything goes well during my absence; I'm only sorry you couldn't come with us to Basle. When I return, you'll go on vacation, my dear friend; that will have to be your consolation.

"I don't plan any postponement of the congress issue, No. 14. Either you or Schöler will get the congress opening and if possible the main speeches on Tuesday, then the continuation by letter and a fairly long wire on Wednesday. The latter will reach Schöler Wednesday evening, so a postponement is *unnecessary*.

"Please run the subscription ad again in No. 13.

"The enclosed is for Knopf [an employe in *Die Welt's* business office]."

The following day, virtually with one foot already on the train—it was the day of his departure for Basle—Herzl sent me a registered letter, written in pencil:

Ischl, 8/23/97

"*Dear Rosenberger,*

"Enclosed are two items to be used only as fillers in case of need.

"Kellner (Leo Rafaels) sent me a good article, 'London Impressions,' which will be the third article, *i.e.,* No. 4 in the Contents. Tell Schöler to print 2,200 copies of [issue] No. 13, of which Knopf should send 400 by parcel post on *Thursday* to the Zionist Congress, Basle.

"3,000 copies are to be printed on the congress issue. I am sending Kollinsky today a postal check for 50 florins for the mailing of No. 13, which he should enter as received.

"Very hurriedly,

"*Yours sincerely,*
"TH. HERZL

"'Hungarian Moods' is to be Budapest correspondence."'

Die Welt's offices had a number of noteworthy visitors during these last days before the congress—delegates *en route* to Basle who were doubtless hoping for an opportunity to meet Herzl face to face. Among them were two distinguished-looking gentlemen from Russia: M. M. Ussischkin, an engineer from Yekaterinoslav, and W. J. Temkin, a rabbi and engineer from Yelizavetgrad. (At that time, I believe, laymen were permitted to perform rabbinical functions in Russia under certain conditions.) What these visitors may have thought upon being greeted in the name of *Die Welt* by a 33-year-old medical student, I cannot say, but I hastened to uphold our reputation by informing them that Herzl and the other members of our staff were either on their way to Basle or already there.

The three days of the congress were days of agonizing suspense for me. The confused mass of manuscripts arriving from Switzerland—largely the texts of reports delivered to the delegates—provided some enlightenment, but I wanted most of all to know if Herzl was satisfied with the way matters were proceeding. At length, on September 1, I received a letter which he had sent two days earlier. It consisted of two parts. The first had been written from Herzl's dictation or on his instructions. The second, less formal in tone, had been written by Herzl himself. The first section read as follows:

"Dear Rosenberger:

"I am sending manuscripts to Schöler the printer just as they are. I can't do the layout here, since I don't have the picture before me. You will have to handle that in a sensible manner according to the sequence of events. This time, Schöler won't be able to make up all the pages on Wednesday, but will have to keep four page forms open; I may run 20 pages this time instead of 16. Thursday morning, I am bringing along to Vienna a whole batch of manuscripts which he will have to have set for me. He should arrange to take on two extra typesetters for those two days, if necessary, so that we can finish on Thursday.

Zion's greetings!"

Then followed Herzl postscript:

"Dear friend, I am also sending you manuscripts that have not been checked. Please go straight to Schöler and look through the manuscripts that have arrived *before they are set*. Be particularly on the alert for *breeches of good taste* and repetitiousness.

"Everything has gone splendidly so far.

"Sincerely yours,

TH. H."

Needless to say, I was overjoyed at the closing sentence. There was no time for celebration, however, for the same mail brought a load of manuscripts: speeches, reports on the debates, "color" stories, and data on the various delegates, newspapermen and guests. I plunged headlong into the sea of material, arranging, sifting, amputating, smoothing out—always trying to govern myself by what Herzl would have wanted.

The same day, September 1, there was further word from Herzl—a telegram for the printer:

"Please arrange for 4 to 6 extra typesetters tomorrow morning. I am bringing remaining manuscripts with me we must furnish tomorrow probably 20 pages—Herzl."

The telegram had been sent at 2:16 that afternoon from the Austrian town of Feldkirch near the Swiss border. I could not help being astounded at the man's driving energy. The very day before had marked the end of the congress, which had taxed his mental and physical powers to the utmost. Yet, here he was already aboard the train, hurrying back to Vienna to make certain that *Die Welt's* congress issue came out on time. Dame Fortune had indeed blessed the Zionist movement when she made Herzl not only a lawyer, writer, orator and diplomat, but also an experienced journalist with an intimate working knowledge of the newspaper business.

As I prepared the Basle material for the printer, I realized that the congress had been a truly impressive demonstration, that the speeches and debates had maintained a level of seriousness and responsibility which would have done honor to any contemporary parliamentary body. Herzl, it need scarcely be said, had been elected president of the congress. He directed the proceedings with the skill, tact and presence of mind of a veteran parliamentarian.

His authoritative personality and natural leadership qualities were enhanced by the experience he had gained in the
years 1891-95 as the *Neue Freie Presse's* reporter in the
French Chamber of Deputies.

The effect Herzl's personality had on the assembled delegates at Basle is illustrated by an incident of which I
learned only some time afterward. As Herzl was mounting
the rostrum amid stormy applause following his election
as president, one of the delegates, yielding to an irresistible
impulse, cried out in Hebrew: "Long like the King!" A
curious episode, one might say. And yet, to anyone who
had known Herzl personally, it would not seem so. For
he was indeed more regal, in both inward spirit and outward bearing, than many a crowned monarch.

After Herzl, I gathered from the manuscripts, it was
Max Nordau who had done the most, through his eloquence and intellect, to make the first Jewish parliament
a success.

The predominant language of the congress was German.
Others were used as well, but German was the mother
tongue of Herzl and a great many of the delegates. Since
most of those from non-German-speaking countries were
also familiar with German, the latter more or less automatically became the official medium of communication.

I have preserved a valuable memento of the congress:
the complete printed list of delegates and guests, which
cites the place of origin and the profession of the 200 men
and women who attended. Among them were a number
of pro-Zionist Christians, including the Reverend Hechler
and Baron M. Manteuffel.

Many of the participants had come long distances in
order to attend the congress. In those days, the journey
to Basle from New York, Jerusalem, Baltimore, Jaffa,

Odessa or Minsk was not the swift airborne jaunt it is today. Dr. Hermann Schapira, the distinguished professor of mathematics at Heidelberg, evinced his devotion to the Jewish-state ideal by making a "pilgrimage" to Basel on foot with six of his students. At the congress, Professor Schapira made several suggestions which were ultimately to yield the most valuable results. It was he who proposed the creation of a Jewish National Fund, based on contributions by rich and poor alike, for the purpose of purchasing land and otherwise furthering the Zionist cause. He was also the first to suggest founding a Jewish university in Jerusalem.

24

HERZL CAME STRAIGHT FROM THE railroad station to the printshop, bringing a sheaf of manuscripts with him. He was the same genial Herzl as always, but there was something new in his face and bearing: He was now a victor returning home—and yet one whom victory had not made haughty.

I can still hear the words as he spoke them: "We had a great success." He said it earnestly, simply, but with a lighting of the eyes. "We" meant all those who had come to contribute their efforts at the Basle congress and all the others who had been there in spirit. Herzl offered no details for the time being and I did not ask questions, for we had a great deal of work ahead of us.

(For some unaccountable reason, one trifling incident of this first day of Herzl's return has remained in my memory; perhaps it is worth a moment's digression. Soon after

our first exchange of greetings, Herzl said to me in a matter-of-fact way: "Rosenberger, I would like your opinion."
Then he turned his neck to me and asked: "Can I still
wear this collar?" He always wore a stiff, white collar
which was separately buttoned onto his shirt; his fondness for it, in fact, had led us to dub it the "Herzl collar."
He was in no sense a dandy, but he liked to be well dressed;
now he wanted to know whether, after the vicissitudes of
a long journey, his collar was still presentable. I carefully
studied the object in question and then delivered my
judgement: "Oh, yes, it still looks fine.")

After I had informed Herzl how things were progressing
with the congress issue of *Die Welt,* we took an explora-
tory walk through the shop. Then, taking a pile of un-
edited manuscripts from the desk, he said: "Let's go over
to the café." Across the street was a small, suburban-type
café; we now hied ourselves to it, laden down with manuscripts and galley proofs. We ordered coffee and rolls, with
Herzl standing treat, and went busily to work. Our activity
stirred no particular interest among the other guests or the
waiter; it was nothing uncommon for the marble-topped
tables of Viennese coffee-houses to be converted into temporary writing-desks. From time to time, Herzl made a
clarifying remark about something that had happened at
Basle. Whenever a manuscript was ready for setting or a
proof had been revised, I took it over to the printshop.

Two days before, acclaimed as a veritable messiah, Herzl
had been pronouncing the closing words before an historic assemblage. Now he was sitting in an unpretentious
little café, diligently and indeed enthusiastically plying
his journalistic trade; the next day, the readers of *Die
Welt* would have an authentic, first-hand report on the
first Zionist congress. "You see," he said to me, *"Die Welt*

is once again proving its worth as an organ that makes us independent of other papers which either ignore the congress altogether or report only what and as much as they please of what happened."

At noon, Herzl interrupted our editorial work and invited me to have lunch with him. A five-minute walk took us to *Das Auge Gottes,* a popular restaurant on the *Nussdorfer Hauptstrasse,* where we sat down at an open-air table. While we ate and afterward, Herzl told me again how pleased he was with the course of the congress and with the promising outlook for the future. In doing so, he made one statement which particularly impressed me and which I often recalled in later years. He reflected silently a few seconds, then looked at me fixedly and said in a lowered voice, as though anxious not to be overheard:

"Don't repeat this to anyone, for they would ridicule you, but it is true nonetheless: At Basle we laid the foundation for our Jewish state."

Of all those who were striving for the realization of the Zionist idea, it was Herzl who believed most firmly that the goal was attainable and would one day be attained. This faith was what gave him his astonishing strength and, at the same time, strengthened and spurred on his followers.

On the way back to the café, Herzl mentioned with particular appreciation and admiration the inestimable contribution which Max Nordau had made, by word and deed, to the success of the congress.

A great deal of work still remained on the issue, and the printing presses were standing ready for the order to roll. "We will provide the gist of what happened at the congress," Herzl said. "Later on, the complete official record will appear separately." Our task was to pack all the most important material into *Die Welt*'s 18 pages of text. We shortened, condensed, omitted, and tried as much as possible to leave the crucial, informative parts intact. The petty mutinies which a handful of rebels had staged in the congress hall, amid nearly unanimous disapproval, were given no more space than they deserved.

Shortly before we finished our editorial chores at the café, a difference of opinion developed between Herzl and me. The point at issue was a short address which Professor Max Mandelstamm of Kiev had delivered toward the end of the congress. After appealing to Herzl to preserve and not yield to discouragement, he had expressed thanks in the name of the congress to those who had helped make it a success:

"But above all and first of all [we thank] that courageous man to whom we are chiefly indebted for the fact that we have gathered here from every country to provide for the future of our people. I refer to the distinguished president of the congress: Dr. Theodor Herzl. (The assembly rises from its seats and breaks into loud cheering.) I believe I am speaking for all members of the congress when I entreat him, fervently entreat him, not to be deterred by the arduous labor he has already done and still has to do, or by the obstacles and annoyances that have beset him and will yet beset him, from completing in the same manner, with the same quality of intellect and the same self-sacrifice, the difficult but rewarding work that he has begun. Long live Dr. Theodor Herzl! (The assembly joins enthusiastically in this cry.)"

When I read Professor Mandelstramm's concluding words, I laid down my pen and leaned back, shaking my head.

"What's the matter?" Herzl asked.

"That passage doesn't sound well at all," I replied.

"Which passage?"

I read it aloud slowly: ". . . annoyances that have beset him *and will yet beset him* . . ."

"What is your objection to that?"

"It's a Cassandra cry," I explained. "He prophesies unpleasant things. Why paint things black?"

"I am prepared for whatever may come," said Herzl.

"Professor Mandelstamm is an excellent doctor, but not even *his* prognoses are infallible," I objected. "Predictions of that sort tend to dishearten, to discourage."

'Discourage?" asked Herzl. "Discourage whom?"

"Some of *Die Welt's* readers."

The evasiveness of my answer was probably noticeable.

"I see," said Herzl teasingly, "that you are supersitious and believe in omens."

The discussion continued a while longer, until finally Herzl said: "I think you attribute too much importance to those few words, but"—and he shrugged slightly—"you do as you see fit. The complete text will appear in the official record anyway."

And so I proceeded to strike the future "annoyances" from the manuscript. I wish I had had the same power to strike them from Herzl's life.

The following day, September 3, with *Die Welt's* congress issue printed and ready for mailing, Herzl informed me that he was leaving for Ischl to spend a little while with his family and gave them a personal account of the events at Basle.

25

HERZL NEVER TRIED TO CONCEAL the fact that, before any particularly important or difficult undertaking, he was in the habit of asking his parents' blessing. From certain indications, I concluded that he had done so before leaving for the Zionist congress in Basle. Now that he was going to Ischl, I strongly suspected that one of his purposes was to thank his mother and father for a blessing which, he felt, had contributed to the favorable outcome of the congress.

On the surface, Herzl's view of the world seemed to be a pantheistic one. Yet, his desire to receive a parental blessing showed that, somewhere deep within him, he believed in the personal God of Jewish monotheism.

Herzl always deleted atheistic remarks from *Welt* articles lest they offend some reader's religious feelings. His innate tact was reinforced by many years' experience on newspapers which made it a policy to exclude anti-religious allusions from their columns. The readers of *Die Welt*, who included a good many orthodox Jews, had to be treated with particular discretion.

But Herzl's distaste for atheistic utterances unquestionably sprang from another source as well—one to which the paragraphs above should offer a clue. Like many a Jew without strong religious feelings, in whom nevertheless a consciousness of "the God of my fathers" still stirs, he may well have said to himself: I will not permit defamation of that which generations upon generations of my fathers and mothers have loved and venerated.

During Herzl's brief stay in Ischl, the postman delivered an item to our office which, upon inspection, I quickly hid from unauthorized eyes. It was an ordinary post card, postmarked "Vienna" and written in an unmistakably feminine hand. It was addressed to "the Hon. Dr. Theodor Herzl." The text side contained neither date nor signature —only the following two stanzas of a poem:

BITTE

Weil' auf mir, du dunkles Auge;
übe deine ganze Macht,
ernste, milde, träumerische,
unergründlich süsse Nacht!

Nimm mit deinem Zauberdunkel
diese Welt von hinnen mir,
dass du über meinem Leben
einsam schwebest für und für!*

It took no great acumen to perceive that a fair admirer of Herzl had chosen this means of declaring her secret passion. (The verse, I recalled from my not-too-distant *Gymnasium* days, was by the Austrian poet Nikolaus Lenau.) Lest the card provide merriment for some irreverent soul, I locked it in my desk drawer.

When Herzl visited the *Welt* office two days later, I gave him some letters which had arrived during his absence, together with the post card. He had just sat down at his desk, and there was no one else in the room. Leafing

---

*ENGLISH TRANSLATION:

ENTREATY

Rest upon me, thou dark eye;
Wield all of thy might,
Earnest, gentle, dreamy,
Fathomlessly sweet night!

Take with thy magic darkness
This world away from me
That lonely, above my life,
Thou may'st eternally hovering be!

through the mail, he finally arrived at the lyrical missive. He read it with a grave expression, and I noticed a slight flush spreading over his face. Then he read it a second time; I suspected that he was trying to decide just how he should behave.

"That's by Le—?" he finally observed in an indifferent tone, leaving the word hanging in air.

"Yes, Lenau," I replied with equal nonchalance.

"Someone is having a joke—someone with lots of time on his hands." He made a motion as though to tear up the "joke," then changed his mind, crumpled the card up and put it in his pocket

Our conversation thereupon turned to editorial matters pertaining to *Die Welt.*

26

THE LEAD ARTICLES WHICH HERZL wrote for *Die Welt* were true labors of love. In *Die Welt,* he could say whatever he pleased, could give free rein to his thoughts and emotions without worrying about what his editor-in-chief might think. For there *he* was the editor-in-chief and the supreme judge of everything that flowed from his pen.

Herzl wrote a great many of his *Welt* articles under the pseudonym "Benjamin Seff." That was, in fact his Hebrew name. It was also a real *nom de guerre,* with which he signed his most militant articles. One of these, which appeared in the issue of October 15, 1897, created something of a sensation that extended even beyond *Die Welt's* regular readership. It was entitled "Mauschel"—a name often applied in Germany and Austria to a vulgar type of Jew. "Mauschel" was a fighting article which gave no quarter. In it, Herzl divided the Jews into two groups: the decent ones and the opposite kind, the Mauschel ilk. In addition to other evil qualities and impulses, Mauschel cherished—and expressed in most treacherous fashion—a profound aversion for the Jewish-state idea. "Mauschel is an anti-Zionist" was the way Herzl's article began, and it closed with a warning that Mauschel would one day get his just deserts.

The connoisseur can distinguish a fine wine under whatever label it may appear. Among the readers of *Die Welt* were the two publishers and editors-in-chief of the *Neue Freie Presse,* Moriz Benedikt and Dr. Bacher, who could recognize a Herzl article regardless of pseudonym. Several days after the appearance of "Mauschel," Herzl told me, Benedikt said to him with a significant smile: "You should get the author of 'Mauschel' to write for the *Neue Freie Presse.*"

* * *

One day in October 1897, Herzl said to me: "Rosenberger, you must help me."

"Gladly," I replied.

"Here is the problem: Feiwel wants to have a humorous wedding newspaper printed for his sister's marriage. He has asked me for a contribution—some verse or something of the sort. I'm not in the mood right now, though; it would mean shifting to a new key. Will you do me a favor and compose something? I'll submit it to the wedding newspaper under my name."

I promised to oblige as quickly as possible. The matter of authorship didn't bother me, since it was a question of helping Herzl out of a mild predicament. Busy as he was, if he wanted to put his signature to the bit of doggerel in order to be spared the necessity of "shifting to a new key," then I had no objection to the innocent deception.

He who makes a tryst with the Muse, however, cannot always set its duration in advance. The couple of lines I had intended to write turned into six verses of six lines each, written in an iambic pentameter whose solemnity rivaled that of an ancient Greek chorus.

The wedding newspaper appeared, together with my contribution. But what were my astonishment and delight at finding that Herzl had provided the following foreword: "Dear Editor:

"In accordance with your kind invitation, I wanted to compose, or at least try to compose, a contribution for the wedding newspaper *Our World*. Since you were harrying me to death and demanding that I produce a poem instanter, whereas it often takes me a year to find a rhyme for a word, I asked my friend Erwin Rosenberger to compose something for me. I wanted to pass it off then as my work. However, Rosenberger played the dastardly trick of writing such a beautiful poem that no one would ever believe it was mine. There is thus nothing left for me but to confess my attempted fraud. The intended wrong has, in any case, been righted. *Our World* is not, let us hope, one in which one becomes bored.

"With wedding greetings and heartiest congratulations,
Yours faithfully,
THEODOR HERZL
'Sister and Brother'
By the falsifier, Erwin Rosenberger"

Then followed my six verses.

I was particularly amused by Herzl's description of me under the title, with its humorous distortion of the facts.

He had masterminded the whole plot, and here he was publicly branding me, innocent, obedient lamb that I was a "falsifier"!

Apropos of this episode, I recall an earlier occasion on which Herzl and I discussed which was more difficult to write, a poem or an article. I had remarked that it was easier to produce a poem, but Herzl disagreed. "I have always felt," he said, "that putting together verses is the more difficult of the two."

*   *   *

Herzl was never a teller of jokes. Unlike many others, he was not given to retailing the latest "funny story" that was making the rounds. Nor, for that matter, did he need to; when the occasion called for it, he could always produce a bit of authentic Herzlian wit that easily held its own with the current quips. In his speeches, on the other hand, he had no objection to using anecdotes to support his rhetorical points.

One of the few occasions on which I recall Herzl repeating someone else's *bon mot* in private conversation was just after the First Zionist Congress. When he returned to Vienna from Basle, he greeted me with a pun coined by one of the delegates: "Baseltov!" (Basel, the German name for Basle, lent itself readily to a play on the popular Jewish expression of congratulations, "Mazeltov!")

*   *   *

Though he often dictated letters, I do not recall ever having seen Herzl dictate one of his *feuilletons* or other literary or journalistic creations. When he wrote, he preferred to sit pen in hand, alone with his thoughts. He was more the contemplative than the declamatory type, and the presence of another person would have interferred with the creative process.

It is true that in the early *Welt* days I often sat near him in his study while he worked on an article. However, I was a companion who did not disturb, who sat there—to all appearances—oblivious of everything about me but the manuscripts and proof-sheets that covered my desk.

27

IN THE FIRST WEEK OF December 1897, Herzl's wife said to me: "Herr Rosenberger, I have a request to make of you, an important request. But it must remain a secret. My husband must know nothing about it . . . You understand?"

The last two words were addressed to the Herzl children's governess, who nodded assent.

"It is to be a surprise for Chanukah, which we are celebrating in the last week of December," Frau Herzl continued in her calm, pleasant manner. Heretofore, she explained, the Herzl family had gathered around a gaily decorated Christmas tree on Christmas eve, so that the children could have the same pleasure as the Gentile children in the neighborhood. From now on, however, her husband wanted things to be different: The Jewish festival of Chanukah was to be celebrated in December instead of Christmas, and the Menorah, the seven-armed candelabrum, was to be lighted instead of the candles on the Christmas tree.

Frau Herzl showed that she was well-informed about the meaning of the eight-day Chanukah festival, about its connection with the priestly family of the Maccabees who had led a heroic struggle against foreign rule in ancient Judea. I also had the impression that one of her main reasons for introducing this historical background into the conversation was to make clear to the Gentile governess why the Christmas tree was being abandoned.

As for the "important request," Frau Herzl wanted me to write a simple little poem for her younger daughter, Trude, to recite on the evening of December 19 before the first Chanukah candle was lighted. It would be a pleasant surprise for the little girl's father.

Trude was at that time about 4 years old. Her older sister, Pauline, was 7. "Perhaps," I suggested, "Pauline would find it easier to memorize and recite the poem."

"We will see," said Frau Herzl. "Either Trudel or Pauline."

In the end, Pauline recited the poem on the first night of Chanukah. Frau Herzl told me afterward that she had carried out her assignment without stumbling and with correct emphasis, and that Herzl had been very pleased.

*   *   *

The incident of the Chanukah poem proved how ready Frau Herzl was to show sympathy and understanding for the new career to which her husband had dedicated himself. Subsequently, she often accompanied him to public Maccabean celebrations and Zionist gatherings. I noted on all these occasions that she attentively followed the speeches and discussion—particularly, of course, when Herzl himself mounted the speaker's platform.

Frau Herzl was pleased and proud at the mighty ovations accorded her husband, but she made no public display of her emotions. I still have a vivid picture of her sitting at Herzl's right among the guests of honor at a Maccabean celebration, simply dressed and charming all who saw or spoke to her with her unassuming, winning manner. Herzl could always appear publicly with his wife, secure in the knowledge that she would look and act in a way that did him credit.

Frau Herzl was also a reader of *Die Welt*. From various remarks I heard her make, moreover, it was apparent that she read it with sound judgment.

She did not have the slightest trace of arrogance or conceit. When she spoke, it was with an unpretentious sincerity of manner. I recall, too, how much common sense and often psychological insight her remarks revealed. One of her most attractive qualities, it always seemed to me, was her calm, even disposition. Everything about her— speech, gestures, manner of walking, and facial expression —suggested a kind of imperturbability. And yet, while placid, she could in no sense be described as a phlegmatic person.

It cannot have been easy for Herzl's wife to take a sympathetic attitude toward the Zionist movement; indeed, that sympathy implied a substantial measure of self-denial. For what Herzl gave in time and devotion to his yearned-for Jewish state, he inevitably took from his family life, his wife and children. His passionate absorption in a political cause could not but distract, and sometimes even blot out, his thoughts of his loved ones. For Frau Julie Herzl, Zionism represented a rival. And it was only her love for her husband that made it possible for her to summon love and understanding for that "rival."

28

FOR SEVERAL DAYS in January 1898, an at-
mosphere of crisis reigned at *Die Welt*: Herzl had resolved
to fight a duel. It all came about in the following manner.

There was living at that time an Austrian archaeologist
and explorer, Dr. Eduard Glaser, who had achieved renown
for his studies in Arabia. In Munich, where he was resting
after his latest expedition, word reached Dr. Glaser that
the Viennese journalist Theodor Herzl had organized a
movement to found a Jewish state in Palestine. The news
interested him, for Palestine came in a general sense
within his own professional purview.

Back in 1890, in fact, Glaser had himself proposed the
creation of a Jewish state—but in southern Arabia rather
than Palestine. This project had come to Herzl's attention
in the summer of 1896, several months before the appearance of his *Judenstaat*. The idea of transplanting the Jews
to southern Arabia was not to his taste, but he felt that
the author of the plan might one day prove a worthwhile
collaborator. "This Glaser," he wrote in his diary on
August 3, 1896, "is a man who should be kept in mind.
In any event, he has considerable knowledge of the East,
and he may even have a talent for military organization."
Before very long, Glaser was to provide more than ample
reason for being "kept in mind."

Toward the end of 1897, as he pondered Herzl's Jewish-
state idea in his Munich retreat, a fantastic thought occurred to Dr. Glaser. Herzl, he decided, was an ally of
England, and it was for her benefit that he wanted to
establish a Jewish state in Palestine. Herzl's creation was
to serve as a "buffer state." Whenever England, whose

sphere of influence extended beyond the Suez Canal to the southern border of Palestine, was threatened from the north—by Tsarist Russia, perhaps—the Jewish state would absorb the first shock of the blow or even altogether prevent a collision of the two hostile powers. Not only that; it would also help promote the disintegration of Turkey and—still acting in England's interest—protect the land route from the eastern shore of the Mediterranean to India. As the end-product of his weighty ruminations, Glaser concluded that Herzl's Jewish-state plan was anti-Turkish, anti-Russian and anti-French, that it would cause a reopening of the so-called "Eastern Question," and that it therefore constituted a threat to world peace.

The noted archaeologist thereupon embodied all these ideas in an article, which he sent to the widely read democratic newspaper, the *Berliner Tageblatt*. The *Tageblatt,* whose editor-in-chief, Arthur Levysohn, was a friend of Herzl's but an anti-Zionist, published it on December 26, 1897 under the title, "Zionism: A Reopening of the Eastern Question." In his article, Glaser informed Herzl's followers that they were "visionaries," "dreamers" and fanatics" who were "intoxicated with Zion." As for their leader, he strongly implied that Herzl was actually conspiring with England. Stripped of all circumlocutions, the article accused Herzl of being a British agent who was luring the Jewish people into a nefarious adventure designed to serve the strategic interests of his employers in London.

That Glaser was fully aware of the gravity of his charge seems almost doubtful. And yet, any accusation, however absurd and far-fetched, will find some willing listeners unless it is promptly answered. Indeed, voices were already being raised here and there on the strength of Glaser's article. The Zionist movement, as well as Herzl's personal honor, was in danger of being gravely compromised. A decisive rebuttal was needed.

On January 4, 1898, the *Berliner Tageblatt* published a reply by Herzl (reprinted in *Die Welt* on January 14) which thoroughly laid bare the fallacy of Glaser's reasoning. The old warrior Max Nordau also entered the lists with a plain-spoken article in the *Tagleblatt*. Describing Glaser's contentious as "Arabian fairy tales" which merited only a smile, Nordau added:

"However, he has made insinuations to which we must at once take vigorous exception. He depicts us as puppets dangling from wires pulled in England. He also intimates that this may not even be an unconscious process, but rather that we are acting deliberately in accordance with secret agreements, that we are intentionally and calculatedly misleading the Jews who trust and follow us in order to make them the tools—and, very shortly, the victims—of selfish English schemes. Why we should engage in such diabolical machinations *Herr* Dr. Glaser very prudently does not say. The only possible reason is sufficiently obvious so that even the most myopic reader can safely be left to discover it for himself. We must be in the pay of the British and selling our Jewish brethren for gold, unless we are fools who don't know what they are doing."

Glaser appears to have been unpleasantly surprised by the Herzl and Nordau articles, though he could hardly have expected his charges to go unanswered. He was particularly displeased, however, by a lead article which appeared in *Die Welt*'s first issue for the year 1898. Entitled "Settling Accounts," it dealt ruthlessly with Glaser's assertions. The author was given only as "Spectator."

Who was "Spectator"? The question was debated back and forth. Since he was clearly a man who knew something about writing and was well-informed into the bargain,

Glaser suspected first Herzl, then Nordau of hiding behind the pseudonym. Glaser's articles had by now ceased to appear in the *Berliner Tageblatt*, where he had evidently worn out his welcome. He was therefore compelled to carry on the polemic under less imposing auspices, in a Viennese Jewish paper known as *Dr. Blochs Österreichische Wochenschrift*. The *Wochenschrift*'s publisher, Dr. Bloch, was clearly as anxious as Glaser to unmask the mysterious "Spectator," who remained the focus of much of the controversy. But *Die Welt* offered the following highly uninformative statement:

"They [Drs. Glaser and Bloch] are tormented by a positively sinful curiosity to know who is lurking behind the pseudonym 'Spectator.' We are accommodating enough to state flatly that neither Dr. Herzl nor Dr. Nordau has ever written under this pseudonym. Naturally, however, the Editors vouch for the contents of the much-quoted article...."

Herzl continued the counter-attack against Glaser in three more articles in *Die Welt*. Then one day, when the battle was at its height, he said to me very calmly:

"I am thinking of challenging Dr. Glaser."

I looked at him, astonished and aghast. He was talking of fighting a duel! Tragic cases in the past flashed through my mind. I thought of Lassalle, Pushkin, Lermontov, all of whom had fallen on the dueling ground—valuable lives, snuffed out prematurely. And now Herzl wanted to risk his precious life, which he had dedicated to so lofty a goal, because of a newspaper squabble.

I shook my head in vigorous disapproval.

"You don't like the idea?" Herzl asked.

"Not a bit," I replied bluntly. If one took every newspaper attack seriously, I pointed out, it would mean fighting a duel every week. When one stakes one's very life, it should be for a cause worthy of the sacrifice. In this instance, I saw nothing that could not be settled by the shedding of ink rather than blood; what could the result of a duel possibly prove? And, made eloquent by my deep concern, I added that the life that was at stake here belonged not to Herzl alone but to the Jewish people.

Herzl listened with a kind of objective attentiveness, as though he was not personally involved in the affair; I could not tell what impression my arguments were making on him. Finally, he changed the subject of conversation.

Two days later, Dr. Siegmund Werner (who since October 1897 had taken Dr. Landau's place as Executive Editor of *Die Welt*) told me that Herzl had advised both him and Schalit, each separately, that he contemplated fighting a duel. Both had been flatly opposed. Werner reported that Herzl had said to him: "Rosenberger made the cruelest remark; he said that my challenge would be regarded as a theatrical gesture." (That had, in fact, been one of my objections.)

Nothing further was heard about the duel. Herzl had obviously been convinced by our unanimous opinion that there was no reason for a final arbitrament by pistols or swords. Instead, he terminated the Glaser controversy with a brief note in *Die Welt* (issue No. 8, 1898), which closed with the words: "We do not find these disputations and allegations sufficiently interesting to prolong the debate further."

And with that silence descended upon the Case of the Buffer State and the gentleman who had so rashly brought it into being.

But what of the mysterious "Spectator" whose article had so infuriated Dr. Glaser? The man behind the pseudonym was Dr. Wilhelm Goldbaum, a member of the *Neue Freie Presse*'s editorial staff, well versed in world politics and other fields, who sometimes wrote lead articles for *Die Welt*.

29

THE FIRST ZIONIST CONGRESS had scarcely ended in the summer of 1897 when Herzl began planning for a second. He was firmly convinced of the need for a periodic convocation of Zionist adherents from all over the world, and the success of his initial effort encouraged him in this belief.

The Second Congress was to be held a year after the first. The task of making it a reality was no easier than it had been before. Once again, opponents of the well-meaning as well as the malicious variety made their appearance; some contented themselves with waggling a warning finger, while others threw every conceivable roadblock in the path of the Congress. But Herzl thrust aside all obstacles, and by the summer of 1898 all was in readiness: The Second Zionist Congress was to be held from August 28 to 31, once more in Basle.

Not long before the Congress, Herzl told me that he wanted me to attend this time and asked whether I thought I could obtain a mandate as delegate. I replied that it would not be difficult. Soon afterward, a friend of mine, Dr. Josef Grünberg, arranged for me to represent the Zionist society in his home town of Podhajce. In addition, I received the following letter on August 20 from the president of the Zionist society in the town of Grybów:

"Honorable Sir:

"On the recommendation of Dr. M. Goldberg, the local Zionist society has chosen you as its delegate to Basle. I therefore respectfully beg you to accept the mandate and plead our cause as political Zionists at the Congress.

Faithfully yours,
SAMUEL GOLDBERG

Grybów, 8/19/98"

Thus, I suddenly found myself representing Zionist societies in two Galician towns at the Basle Congress. I have never been in Podhajce or Grybów either before or since, nor, for that matter, have I ever been in Galicia. The Congress rules, however, permitted an organization which was not sending one of its own members as a delegate to nominate a non-resident.

I was a cog, however small, in the parliamentary machinery which Herzl had created to further the cause of a Jewish state. I did not expect to take part in the debates—I would leave that to persons older and wiser than myself—but I would be able to cast my vote and thus make my contribution toward Congress decisions.

I also had another and more influential function to perform: As a reporter for *Die Welt,* I could make known the Congress's accomplishments and help to arouse interest in its objectives. *Die Welt* was also to be represented in the press gallery by Dr. Siegmund Werner. J. Schalit and Moritz Zobel were to remain behind in the Vienna office.

My dual status made me the possessor of two credential cards: the yellow delegate's card and the greenish-blue press card. There was also a pink card for congress guests. Designed by the painter M. Okin, it showed a symbolic picture: the Wailing Wall in Jerusalem, with mourning

figures in the foreground; and next to it the new life
burgeoning out of the ruins—workers in the field, a man
sowing who vaguely resembled Herzl, dancing children,
peacefully grazing cattle, and in the background, encircled
by a halo, a hill with what appeared to be the remains
of a castle, presumably intended to suggest Mount Zion.

Herzl, truly the perfect "boss," told me that I needn't
rush back to my desk at *Die Welt* when the congress was
over: "Look around a bit in Switzerland, in Munich;
don't hurry your trip home."

For my expenses, he had 100 gulden (florins) issued to
me from the office cash-box. That amounted to about 210
francs (or $40) and was an opulent sum, considering its
purpose. At the time, I gave no thought to the ultimate
source of the money; I had no idea to what extent *Die
Welt*'s treasury might possibly be fed from Herzl's private
funds. At that age, financial matters—including those of
our magazine—preoccupied me little or not at all; what
interested me was the contents of *Die Welt*'s 16 pages. It
never occurred to me that the money Herzl was spending
for Zionist purposes might be jeopardizing his own financial position.

With a parting "See you in Basle!" I took leave of Herzl.
He made no attempt to give me directives on how I should
report the congress.

It was my first journey beyond the borders of Austria-
Hungary. Happily, it was attended by none of the passport
formalities which nowadays complicate the life of a
traveler. As far as I recall, the only documents I carried
were a third-class tourist's ticket booklet issued by a Viennese travel agency and, as all-purpose identification, my
university attendance book. (In the hope that I might
some day be able to complete my medical studies, I had

continued to register each semester, although I had not entered a lecture hall or a hospital ward since joining the editorial staff of *Die Welt*.)

I spent my first night in Basle at a rather modest hotel. After that, the congress's housing committee arranged for me to lodge with a local Jewish family.

The morning after my arrival, a Friday, I went to the Casino Hall, where the congress was to be held. It was empty except for a man standing on a ladder, pounding vigorously at the wall with a hammer. His back was turned to me, but the black-clad figure struck me as familiar. . . . Sure enough, it was Hechler—the Reverend William Henry Hechler, chaplain of Her Britannic Majesty's Embassy in Vienna. He was not one to miss the congress.

Stepping closer, I found that he was engaged in nailing a large map of Palestine to the wall. After we had exchanged greetings, he explained: "It is written: The nations will prepare the land for you." He delivered this brief pronouncement with a meaningful look, then drove another nail into the wall.

Good old faithful Hechler! "The nations," of course, meant the non-Jew nations. And Hechler, the non-Jew who would have thrust his hand into the fire to show his faith in the ancient prophecies, wanted at least symbolically to prepare the land for the Jews.

Saturday morning, a few minutes after 8, I visited Herzl in his hotel room after having first been assured that he had been up for some time. He was sitting at his desk, working on the speech which was to open the first session of the congress the following day. I knew that he had been preparing drafts of the speech for some months already; now he was applying the finishing touches and adding tributes to Zionist comrades who had passed away since the last congress. But he was also incorporating an account of an incident of the previous day which, trivial though it might appear, had made a deep impression on him. His voice was filled with emotion as he told me what happened; here is how he described it to the delegates the next day:

"... And we received the first token of the hospitality which this free city is affording us. The day before yesterday, on St. Jacob's Day, the troops were returning from the festival in the evening.... They were marching past our congress building. Then one of our estimable ladies waved her handkerchief in greeting, and that was the signal for a demonstration which we will surely never forget. As they went by, the troops saluted our people, who were cheering them, and a new and unexpected cry surged up from the street: 'Hurrah for the Jews!' ... Many a one among us may have felt the tears welling up in his eyes. At such a moment, one can lose the composure one has learned to maintain under oppression of all kinds, under the most unjust accusations."

I thought about this episode on the way back from my visit to Herzl and found that I could not fully share his joy at what had happened. The good citizens of Basle had shouted "Hurrah for the Jews!" and for that they had earned our gratitude and esteem; it would not be forgotten. And yet, it seemed to me, a bitter note was inevitably mixed in with the feelings of gladness among the Jews who were there. For how sad it was that this shout of greeting, which would have been taken for granted by any other people, should seem so precious and noteworthy to the Jews.

In Herzl's eyes, the demonstration of sympathy had been largely inspired by the Zionist banner fluttering from the balcony of the congress building. He felt that the flag with the star of Zion had been a catalyst that drew the Jews and the citizens down below closer together.

* * *

While in Herzl's hotel room, I had noticed that he had clothes laid out of the sort one wears on solemn occasions: a gleaming black top-hat and a long full-dress jacket that reached down below the knees. He was preparing to attend Saturday-morning services in the Basle synagogue.

I wrote a short report for *Die Welt* on the services. The large temple was filled to overflowing. The foreign Jews who had come to attend the congress wore blue-and-white rosettes with a star of David, which stood out against their black costumes. The local Jews, who had given the Zionist visitors a hearty welcome, were also present in large numbers. The synagogue was a beautiful tall structure in Moorish style; colored Arabesques covered the walls right up to the two mighty domes, from which golden stars set in a blue background looked down upon the stars of Zion below. When the Torah was taken out, Herzl was called to the altar.

To what extent Herzl's visit to the synagogue sprang from a religious need, and to what extent it represented a concession to the religious feelings of Congress delegates, is a question I will not go into here. At all events, his attendance at the services did not fail to impress the more devout among his followers.

The following day, Sunday, August 28, 1898, the Second Zionist Congress opened. The atmosphere in the hall was almost like that of a religious festival—a festival at once joyful and solemn. When Herzl appeared on the rostrum, he was met by a tumultuous roar which could not have been greater if he had been one of the Chosen of Israel returned to earth, clad in the robes of a High Priest. The delegates rose from their seats, waving, cheering and stamping their feet; the ovation seemed as though it would never end. During a brief lull, Herzl turned to greet some of the delegates seated on the platform, but the moment he turned back to the gathering the applause burst forth again.

At last, Herzl began to speak, but his address was interrupted by repeated salvos of applause. When he proclaimed his readiness to carry the battle to the enemies of Zionism, his listeners' enthusiasm knew no bounds. The conclusion of the speech set off a new ovation. Delegates rushed to the platform to congratulate the speaker and shake his hand; in the gallery, the guests leaned over the railing and waved hats and handkerchiefs.

From my place at the press table, I had a good view of the hall. Every seat was filled. Among the delegates and guests one could see men and women; graybeards, striplings and all the gradations of age in between; Western European Jews in modern dress and Eastern European Jews in orthodox garb, with long black caftans and black skullcaps. Every racial strain which the Jewish people had acquired in its millennial wanderings seemed to be represented in the hall. The Congress was, among other things, an ethnologist's paradise.

*　*　*

On the second day of the Congress, an incident occurred which brought the Russian delegates, and with them the entire Zionist movement, to the very brink of disaster. The previous day had been marked by a sensational development on the international scene: The Tsar of Russia had issued an appeal for a peace conference. In the name of peace, he pointed out, the great powers were arming on an unprecedented scale, spending vast sums on engines of destruction which were rendered obsolete by new developments in military science almost as fast as they were produced. The situation could only end in catastrophe. Therefore, the Tsar proposed that a conference be held to consider means of halting the arms race and averting the calamity that threatened mankind.

Monday morning, at the Zionist Congress in Basle, delegate Aschkenasi-Delines rose and read the text of the Tsar's spectacular peace message. But before the speaker could proceed with his own observations, a veritable explosion of noisy indignation occurred in the section of the hall where the Russian delegates were sitting. Loud cries of "Shame!" and "Enough!" were heard from the Russians, while from other parts of the hall came answering shouts of "Quiet!"

Needless to say, the protesting delegates were not militarists. Their anger was not directed against the peace proposal, but against its author. It was the word "Tsar" which had brought them up in arms. They were demonstrating against the Tsarist regime, which had oppressed the Jews of Russia for so long and brought many of them violent death at the hands of pogromists. Let the Tsar create decent, humane conditions in his own land, they were saying in effect, before he sets out to solve the world's problems.

During all this, I had stopped writing and my eyes were wandering back and forth between Herzl and the center of the disturbance. Herzl had risen to his feet on the platform, a look of deep concern on his face; he knew that it was a critical moment. Carried away by understandable emotions, the demonstrators had failed to realize that they were compromising the entire Congress in the eyes of the Russian Government, creating the impression that it was a hotbed of anti-Tsarist intrigue. The consequences could

be grave. The plight of the Russian Jews would become
worse than ever, and Zionism would unquestionably be
banned in Russia. Russian delegates would be unable to
attend future congresses, and the effort to create a Jewish
state would henceforth have to contend with bitter opposi-
sition from the Tsar. As for the Russian delegates now in
Basle, who could say what their fate would be when they
returned home?

All these thoughts were racing through Herzl's mind as
he stood on the platform. But he swiftly showed that he
was master of the situation. Employing all of his authority
and skill, he prevailed upon the hotheads to listen while
Max Nordau addressed the Congress. Nordau, temperately
yet cogently, explained to the Russian delegates what a
dangerous game they were playing; then he introduced two
motions which delegate Aschkenasi-Delines had been unable to read amid the general hubbub. These proposed,
first, that the Congress express approval of the Tsar's
initiative on behalf of a peace conference, and, second,
that a memorandum be addressed to the participants in
such a conference, calling upon them to let justice be done
at last to the Jewish people and to support the latter's
return to the land of their fathers.

Nordau's speech, together with a statement by another
delegate, Dr. Bodenheimer, and an effective concluding
word by Herzl, calmed the troubled waters. Before all
those in the hall were fully aware of what had happened,
the brief outburst among the Russian delegates was over.
Herzl had successfully piloted the Congress past the suddenly appearing reef; a stern warning note, hastily scrib-
bled and sent to the Russians, had been a decisive factor.
Indeed, so effective had been Herzl's handling of the whole
episode that the motion welcoming the Tsar's peace message was adopted unanimously by the Congress.

As a reporter, I now faced a difficult decision. *Die Welt* had subscribers in Russia, and it could be assumed that the Tsar's police scrutinized it regularly for possible objectionable material. If I wrote a factual account of the incident that had just occurred, it might have all the tragic consequences referred to above. I finally decided to violate my journalistic conscience and wrote an innocuous report which contained not a word about the brief flurry among our Russian comrades.

* * *

After Herzl, Max Nordau was the most respected figure at the Basle Congress. His standing was high among those in the hall, and his international fame as a writer lent prestige to the gathering in the outside world.

Nordau had been living in Paris since 1880 and, like Herzl, was versed in all the refinements of French parliamentary procedure. He was therefore eminently qualified to direct the proceedings of the Congress when, as vice president, he occasionally took over the chair from Herzl.

His name, his physical appearance, his behavior at the Congress, and his oratorical gifts won Nordau the respect of all those present. Even the rabbis and the orthodox Jews, with that handsome, white-bearded philosopher's face before them, could forgive for the moment his many attacks on "the religious lie" and his refusal to attend synagogue services while in Basle. The son of Rabbi Gabriel Südfeld, they told themselves, had found his way back to Judaism—if not by the faith of religion, then by that of national consciousness.

At the Second Zionist Congress just as at the First, Nordau offered the delegates a masterly exposition of the over-all situation of the Jewish people. What he presented was, by and large, a melancholy picture; only in Holland,

Belgium, Italy, Switzerland and the Scandinavian countries did the Jews find justice and sympathy. Nordau neither varnished the truth nor painted it in overly dark hues, and the reactions of the delegates from the various countries attested to the accuracy of his portrayal.

In my report to *Die Welt,* I tried to do justice to the impression which Nordau made on those who heard him. He held his audience completely spellbound; only Herzl exerted a similar power. Such was Nordau's artistry on the rostrum that one might have thought he had spent decades in a parliamentary chamber, taking passionate part in every debate. Every syllable, every letter was sharply enunciated, and the inflection conveyed the subtlest nuances. Nordau keyed his tempo at any given moment to the particular theme he was treating. One moment, the words would follow one another in measured, leisurely fashion; the next, they would pour forth in a swift stream. And always they were accompanied by the natural, appropriate gesture.

* * *

One episode at the Basle Congress is connected with the origin of Herzl's novel, *Altneuland* ("Old-Newland"). After the morning session on the third day of the Congress, a luncheon was held for the press at the Hotel Braunschweig. Most of the reporters were there as well as a number of distinguished figures from the worlds of literature, scholarship and religion, including Herzl, Nordau, Bernard Lazare, and the Rev. Dr. Moses Gaster Hakham of the Sephardic congregation in London. There were some thirty guests in all.

Toasts were offered, and tongues began to loosen as the wine flowed. Herzl acted very much *en famille,* a journalist among journalists; for the moment, his high station as

Congress president was forgotten. Inevitably, he was called upon to say a few words. And thereupon he proceeded to violate a principle to which he invariably remained faithful: that one does not divulge literary plans in advance, particularly if one's professional colleagues are present.

In the course of a humorous talk, Herzl declared: "I have already had a try at every type of writing and journalism—with just one exception: I have yet to write a real novel. However, I plan to correct that deficiency soon. It is going to be a Zionist novel." He then briskly outlined the plot of a novel dealing with the future—the book which later received the title, *Altneuland*.

Back in Vienna not long afterward, Herzl asked me one day: "Rosenberger, do you remember my discussing, at the journalists' luncheon in Basle, an idea for a Zionist novel set in the future?

"I remember it very well," I replied.

"Jot down for me what I said at that time," Herzl then requested. "I was in a buoyant mood, and I would like to know how much I disclosed."

I had listen very intently to what Herzl said at the Basle luncheon, and, since I was virtually a total abstainer, my wits had been unclouded by the copiously flowing spirits. The next day, therefore, I brought Herzl something rather close to a verbatim transcript of his remarks about the projected novel. Since then, I have often wondered: Would *Altneuland* ever been written if Herzl had not revealed its main ideas that day before an audience of newspapermen and writers?

For a year after the luncheon episode, there was no word as to whether Herzl, amid all his other work, was writing a novel as well. I was in daily contact with him, but I was not bold enough to bring up the subject and he himself never referred to it.

In the summer of 1899, Herzl returned from another Zionist Congress in Basle—the Third, which was held August 15-18. I had no idea whether he had said anything about his novel, and, if so, what; just as two years earlier, I had remained behind to put out the Congress issue of *Die Welt*. Then, on August 29, the office boy brought me a short note from Herzl's home:

"Vienna, August 29, 1899

"Dear Rosenberger,

"Regarding my novel, please be sure to print nothing but the enclosed lines.

Sincerely yours,

TH. H."

The "enclosed lines," which were published in *Die Welt* of September 1, were as follows:

"As Dr. Herzl stated in Basle, he is working on a novel depicting conditions in the projected new commonwealth twenty years after its creation."

At last, Herzl's novel was an acknowledged fact. There was no indication of how he had come to make the disclosure in Basle, and I did not ask. The important thing was that he had now formally announced in print that a novel was taking shape in the study at No. 6 *Berggasse*.

Realizing that I still remembered everything he had said the year before at the journalists' luncheon and might be tempted to offer the reader a few further details about his book, Herzl had asked me to print nothing but his bare announcement. He was proceeding on the very sound principle that the reading public should be allowed to sniff the tempting aroma emanating from the kitchen, but should not be told too far in advance precisely what dish was being served up.

As yet, the book had no title—or so I thought. As it happened, Herzl had made the following entry in his diary on August 30, the day after he sent me the announcement:

"Today, as I was jolting along in the streetcar on my way out to Währing [the section of Vienna where Herzl lived], the title for my Zionist novel occurred to me: *Altneuland*. A borrowing from the name of the *Altneuschul* in Prague. The word will some day be famous."

Herzl hesitated at first to make the title known to the public—whether because he did not want to talk too much about his novel, or because he wished to avoid personal publicity, or because he had not definitely decided to use that title. It was not until seven weeks later, in the middle of October, that he handed me a piece of paper with the remark: "This goes in the 'World Chronicle' column." On it were barely three-and-a-half handwritten lines:

"The Zionist novel about the future, on which Dr. Theodor Herzl is now working, is entitled *Altneuland*."

Once this appeared, there was no turning back; everyone now knew that the novel not only was being written but had even acquired a title. In fact, Herzl printed the item precisely because he wanted to cut off his own retreat, to obligate himself to complete the project. Then he would not succumb to the temptation, whether for lack of time or another reason, to consign the unfinished manuscript to an eternal resting place in some dark corner of his desk.

"The word will some day be famous," Herzl had written in his diary, referring to the title of his novel. A rather self-assured remark, it might seem, but it proved to be among those of his prophecies which ultimately came true.

Herzl was highly pleased with the results of the Second Zionist Congress. That was apparent both from the way he looked and from what he said. And it was not just the "concrete" results, but equally the imponderable "moral" gains, that gratified him.

After the First Congress, the opinion had been widespread that the Jewish parliament's premiere performance would prove to be its last. Now, with the holding of the Second Congress, those who held this view had been given the lie. Indeed, if a second congress was possible, then why not many more? Zionism's prestige had risen perceptibly.

For Herzl, the Second Congress was a kind of military review. He saw that he had followers and that they were worth their salt; the quality of the speeches and debates showed this. This time, too, the Congress participants could truly call themselves "delegates," for each of them was the duly elected spokesman for some group and his mandate had been carefully checked and approved by the Congress's credentials committee. At the First Congress, there had been a good many delegates who represented no one's views but their own. But now Herzl could look down from his president's chair upon the representatives of thousands of men and women who stood behind him and the Jewish-state idea. Now he was indeed the leader of a "movement."

* * *

Indicative of the public stir created by the Second Zionist Congress was a long article that appeared in the *Neue Preussische Zeitung* of Berlin on September 10, 1898. The paper was popularly known as the *Kreuzzeitung,* since there was an Iron Cross symbol, ringed by the legend "Forward with God for King and Country," between the words *"Preussische"* and *Zeitung"* of the title. Widely read in Germany, the *Kreuzzeitung* was strongly clerical

and ultra-conservative. It had never been accused of excessive fondness for the Jews. Yet, the first paragraph of its
September 10 article clearly showed that, after the second
Basle congress, Zionism had become a force to be reckoned
with:

"At the end of last month, as our readers know, the
Zionists held a congress in Basle for the second time; they
have set themselves the task of rallying the Jewish people
on a national basis and creating 'a legally secured, publicly
recognized home' for them in the land of their fathers.
Until now, these efforts to establish a Jewish state in
Palestine have been scoffed at; the curious scheme was
thought to be merely the brainchild of a few Jewish
visionaries. But the course of the Basle congress has shown
that the 'Zionist' organization has progressed further than
was supposed and that . . . the colonization of Palestine is
to be begun shortly with the help of a Jewish National
Bank capitalized in the amount of 40 million marks. Consequently, the congress can claim the right to be taken
seriously."

As a result of the Second Congress, a number of prominent newspapers throughout the world thrust the Jewish-
state movement from its previous semi-obscurity into the
light of publicity. The overwhelming majority of them
did so in a sympathetic rather than antagonistic spirit.

30

AT THE SECOND ZIONIST CONGRESS,
a number of women sat as fully accredited
delegates. Today, the fact would not even be worth mentioning, but things were very different back then. Only

a year before, a delegate to the First Congress had risen
to ask the chair whether women were entitled to vote and
had received the reply from Herzl: "The ladies are of
course highly honored guests, but they will not take part
in the voting." Sixty years ago, the old Latin injunction
was still largely in force: *"Mulier taceat in ecclesia"*—"Let
the woman be silent in public assembly."

Yet, the Second Congress in 1898 repudiated this doc-
trine of female inferiority. Women had rendered notable
services to the Zionist movement and had been delegated
by various Zionist groups to represent them at Basle.
Women's hats, generously beribboned in the current style,
were to be seen throughout the Congress hall. At the final
session, a woman delegate, Frau Ellmann, expressed her
gratitude for the Congress's stand:

"The Jewish woman has been given a seat and a voice
in the councils of the men. This right which has been
granted her imposes upon her the duty to do all in her
power to further our great work."

Not surprisingly, the policy of female equality met with
Herzl's wholehearted approval. What did seem rather remarkable to me, however, was the attitude of the more
religious members of the Congress, especially the orthodox
rabbis from Eastern Europe. In their synagogues at home,
they would have been quick to object if a woman took
a seat among the men rather than in the separate latticed
section provided for her sex. Yet, they raised no outcry
whatever when men and women were seated side by side
at Basle. The blue-and-white Zionist banner fluttering over
the Congress hall had its unifying effect.

A festive gathering of delegates on the evening of August
29 was marked by a lyrical tribute to the Congress's distaff
participants. Delegate Jacques Bahar read a French poem

which he had written. *"Respectueusement dédié à Madame Bernard Lazare,"* it celebrated the glory of Jewish women down through the ages, their heroism in times of travail, their martyrdoms, their love for their people. It invoked the names of Esther, Deborah, Miriam, Rachel and Rebecca, and closed with the passionate cry: *"O juive, ma déesse!"*—"O Jewess, my goddess!"

* * *

German was the official language at the Second Congress just as at the First. Speeches delivered in Hebrew, Russian, French or English were translated into German afterward.

The privileged position of German at the congresses, and in the Zionist movement generally, resulted chiefly, of course, from the fact that it was Herzl's mother tongue and the one in which he preferred to express himself. His pamphlet *Der Judenstaat,* which had contributed so mightily to the birth of Zionism, was written in German. So, too, was *Die Welt,* which served as the more or less official Zionist organ. The Zionist Action Committee set up to assist Herzl had its headquarters in Vienna, and its statements and directives were issued in German. Moreover, the Jewish university students of Vienna, who had been among the first to rally to Herzl's side, now formed a kind of shock troop engaged in carrying the Zionist idea to the Jewish people. The familiarity of many foreign Jews with German made our task easier; at *Die Welt,* I was often astonished, upon opening an envelope adorned with the Russian double-eagle, the Bulgarian lion, or the bearded countenance of the King of Rumania or an American President, to find a letter written in good German and in the correct German *Schrift.*

Of course, many of the Russian and other Eastern European delegates at the congresses lacked intimate knowledge of modern German. However, they all spoke Yiddish, which is basically a survival of medieval German, so that communication was not a great problem.

At the Second Congress, some of the delegates who spoke French, English and other languages staged a brief revolt against the German linguistic monopoly. The insurgents won certain concessions, but German remained the chief medium of communication.

*   *   *

On August 27, the local Zionist organization in Basle arranged a concert in honor of the Second Congress. All eleven selections were heartily applauded—the *Fantasie* from Wagner's *Tannhäuser* no less than the others. Listening to this tribute to a musical genius who had also been a notorious anti-Semite, I could not help wondering whether an audience of anti-Semites would have been equally generous to the Jewish composers Halévy and Meyerbeer, whose works were also represented on our program that evening!

31

HERZL AND I were standing in Bergmann's printshop one day, watching as page after page of *Die Welt* issued in stately procession from the press. Herzl gazed for a time at the rhythmic movements of the machine, glanced around the press-room, and then turned to me with the remark:

"Zionism is Attila in reverse; wherever it sets foot, shoots burst from the ground."

Of King Attila, whose Huns had once laid waste much of Europe, it was said that no blade of grass grew again where his horse had set foot. Herzl's words referred to the printshop of Siegmund Bergmann, to which *Die Welt* had taken its business in February 1898. Bergmann, a Jew, had just moved to Vienna from Reichenberg in Bohemia; his *"Industrie"* shop was located at No. 11 *Schlösselgasse*. At first, business had been slow. Once *Die Welt* became his customer, however, Bergmann began to prosper. He received orders from the Zionist Action Committee, from various Zionist societies, etc., and he was able to enlarge his establishment. Among other things, the *"Industrie"* shop printed the official record of the Zionist Congress, Herzl's pamphlet *Der Baseler Congress* (dealing with the First Congress), and the book editions of his drama *Das Neue Ghetto* ("The New Ghetto") and his comedy *Unser Käthchen* ("Our Katy"), as well as the stock certificates and prospectus of the Jewish Colonial Trust. As far as Bergmann's printshop was concerned, therefore, it could indeed be said that Zionism had proved to be "Attila in reverse."

*   *   *

Another time, as we were watching the printing press do its work, Herzl pointed to the pages coming out. "You see that black spot there," he said. "That little round thing can sometimes help ruin a newspaper publisher."

He was speaking of the printed "newspaper stamp." At that time, all periodicals had to pay a tax for permission to appear—a survival from the days when governments had imposed all sorts of restrictions on the press. The "newspaper stamp" showed that the tax had been paid. For its first few years, *Die Welt,* like other Austrian papers, carried the round printed symbol on its first page, next to the title: the Austrian double-eagle, with the words "Imperial Newspaper Stamp."

* * *

Among his other contributions to the *Neue Freie Presse,* Herzl wrote humorous fillers for the Sunday edition which appeared in the news columns rather than in the *feuilleton* section. These brief items, which were often choice specimens of Herzlian wit, were always signed with a pseudonym, such as "Kunz" or "X.Y., Local Reporter."

One day, I said to Herzl: "It's a shame these fillers don't carry your signature instead of just a pen-name."

"Impossible!" he replied. 'What would *** and *** and *** say"—and he named several prominent foreign Zionists—"if they saw my name signed to those jokes. I can't afford to be seen playing the wag."

And so the author's vanity had to yield to the Zionist leader's prestige.

* * *

During the time I worked under him, Herzl rarely assumed the role of mentor. The few journalistic "tips" he gave me came, for the most part, in my first months on *Die Welt.*

"Learn to avoid the lyrical tone," he said to me once in his well-meaning, friendly tone"; it was one of the qualities that lent charm to his *feuilletons.* What he meant was that lyricism might seem out of place in a largely political paper like ours. And yet, perhaps I could be pardoned for feeling that *Die Welt,* which throbbed with longing for the land of Biblical legend, for the fields through which the Jordan flows and where Ruth once stood amid the alien corn, had as much of lyricism as of politics in it.

"One should not strain for a joke," Herzl said to me another time. "It will come by itself."

Once, when we were working on *Die Welt* in the *Berggasse,* he took a bright-blue-covered paperbound book off the shelf and handed it to me with the jocular warning:

"Don't use it as a model!"

It was his own *Buch der Narrheit* ("Book of Folly"), a 266-page collection of gay sketches and stories published in 1888. Herzl's wife, who was present, seemed astonished at this disparagement of a book of which she thought highly and had enjoyed reading. By contrast with *Der Judenstaat,* however, the *Buch der Narrheit* seemed to its author an utterly insignificant work.

On another occasion, Herzl offered me the advice: "Read Tacitus!" I nodded my head, but said nothing. The reason for this lack of enthusiasm was a curious one. Lodged in some recess of my memory was a passage I had once read which had gravely shaken my faith in the great Roman historian's credibility. As I recalled, Tacitus had made the absurd assertion that the Jews in their temples worshipped . . . an ass! Hence, I accepted Herzl's advice with thanks but made no effort to act on it.

Herzl also advised me once, in the forceful tone he sometimes adopted in such matters: "Read the *Letters of Junius!*" He was referring to a famous series of political letters, of still unknown authorship, which appeared in a London newspaper in 1769-72 under the pseudonym "Junius." It so happened that I had a German translation in my library which I had glanced at occasionally but never really read. Here again, however, Herzl's advice fell on barren soil; I never did take the time to read "Junius."

32

IN THE SUMMER OF 1899, Herzl was in Holland. During May, June and July, The Hague was the scene of an international peace conference—a conference resulting from the spectacular appeal by Tsar Nicholas II which had had such an explosive effect at the Second Zionist Congress the previous summer. Herzl's purpose in journeying to the Dutch capital was to establish contacts with Russian statesmen attending the conference; this he hoped to achieve with the aid of Baroness Suttner, a noted Austrian pacifist and author and a sincere friend of the Jewish people. Through the Russian delegates at The Hague, he hoped then to gain access to Government ministers in St. Petersburg and perhaps even the Tsar himself. His object in all this was twofold: to prevail upon the Tsar to take the Zionist movement under his protection, and to obtain relief for the 4,500,000 Russian Jews, most of whom led an utterly wretched existence.

The Hague Conference also provided an excellent opportunity for propaganda on behalf of the Jewish-state idea. Here, too, Baroness Suttner could be very helpful, and Herzl spared no expense to achieve the desired end. In May, while still in Vienna, he wrote in his diary:

"Baroness Suttner wrote to me, asking that I intercede at the *Neue Freie Presse* to have her sent to the peace conference at The Hague with a 'contribution' of 1,000 florins. The publishers would not do it. I then offered her 1,000 florins to go for *Die Welt* and interview the main people at the conference on behalf of Zionism. She accepted. Thus, we have brought Zionism before the assembled powers of

Europe, without offending Turkey and infringing on her rights. I plan to go to The Hague myself in June and try to make the peacemakers' acquaintance in Baroness Suttner's drawing room."

A thousand florins was a substantial sum of money, but Herzl never stinted when it was a question of advancing the Zionist cause. Indeed, not long afterward, in August 1899, he wrote in his diary that his personal expenditures on behalf of Zionism had already exceeded 50,000 florins. The ideal to which he had dedicated himself was carrying him perilously close to financial ruin.

Before leaving for The Hague, Herzl asked me to divulge his address only in the most urgent cases, since he did not want to be bothered with letters. In addition to all the personal contacts he hoped to make in the Dutch capital, he had to draft a speech to be delivered later in London.

While in The Hague, Herzl stayed at the Hotel Kurhaus, an expensive establishment in the well-known North Sea resort of Scheveningen. His social and literary position normally required him to maintain a certain standard of living, and in this case he had to be particularly careful in his choice of lodgings. He had come to Holland with the intention of mingling on equal terms with statesmen and diplomats, as spokesman for a movement which hoped to buy an entire province from the Sultan of Turkey and which, at that very moment, was engaged in founding a bank and hence was seeking substantial credits. Under the circumstances, he could scarcely put up at some second-class inn.

On his very first day in The Hague, Herzl was introduced by Baroness Suttner to a prominent Russian, Johann von Bloch, a member of the advisory committee of the

Ministry of France. Born into a Warsaw Jewish family, Bloch had made a career as an industrialist and economist which had brought him high in the personal favor of the Tsar. He was the author of a four-volume work, *Russia's Finances,* as well as a six-volume study, entitled *War,* which was pacifistic in tendency. At the time Herzl met him, Bloch was 63; he had converted to Christianity many years before. When at length Herzl brought the conversation around to Zionism, Bloch promised that, if the circumstances were favorable, he would try to obtain an audience with the Tsar for Herzl. He also declared that it might be possible to induce the Tsar to issue a rescript favoring Zionism. Thus, Herzl's journey to The Hague had not been without result.

On June 17, Herzl left for Paris. His London speech, which he hoped would bring added support for the movement and especially for the new bank, the "Jewish Colonial Trust," was scheduled for the end of the month. It was to be merely a "standard speech," as Herzl expressed it, but not a word of it was as yet down on paper. The Hague, with the excitement of the conference and the *soirées* at Baronett Suttner's, had scarcely been the place for Herzl to collect his thoughts. Fortunately, however, he knew of a quiet retreat which had already proved its worth as a stimulus to literary creation—the Hotel Castille in Paris, where four years before he had written *Der Judenstaat.*

Among other things, Herzl visited an automobile show while in Paris. His interest was partly personal, for he had once told me that he hoped to own a small car when a moderate-priced one became available. Like everything else he thought and did, however, the visit was also linked with the great, consuming mission of his life: Zionism. He was intensely interested in the rapid advance of modern trans-

portation, to which he had already assigned an important
role in the future Jewish state.

In London, Herzl found obstacles to be overcome and
various irksome complications. In the end, however, his
efforts were crowned with success. On June 28, I received
a wire from the British capital: "IF NO WIRE TO CON-
TRARY BY TOMORROW NOON PLEASE PRINT
FOLLOWING DISPATCH BOLD FACE BOARD OF
DIRECTORS HAS DECIDED TO PROCEED TO AL-
LOTMENT OF SHARES THUS OUR BANK HAS
DEFINITELY BEEN FOUNDED."

I could well imagine the joy and relief with which Herzl
had written the last sentence: "Thus, our bank has definitely been founded." The Jewish Colonial Trust was a
vital new step toward the creation of a Jewish state, which
would further discomfit the scoffers and breathe new confidence into our supporters. And, it might be added, Herzl
had contributed not only his usual tireless energy but
also a substantial sum of money to its founding.

The bank's prospectus, statements, subscription appeals,
etc. stressed that it had been established "as the financial
instrument through which the ideas of Zionism are to be
put into practice." One statement cited as one of its purposes "the acquisition of land for the founding of new
settlements on a publicly and juridically secured basis."
The bank's capital amounted to £2 million divided among
2 million shares of stock valued at £1 each. The 20-odd-
member board of directors was, of course, headed by Herzl.

The prospectus made it clear that the "founders' shares"
issued to the members of the board would not provide a
source of profit. They merely enabled the board to exercise
legal control over the bank's affairs and see to it that
"the objectives of Zionism, for whose furtherance and de-

velopment the company [*i.e.,* bank] was founded, are always kept in the foreground." Herzl was almost painfully concerned with avoiding any suspicion that he wished to turn Zionism to his own material advantage. And we know what the material fruits of his Zionist endeavors were: the steady deterioration of his financial position.

*   *   *

Several days after the joyful news about the bank, I received another wire from Herzl which filled me with foreboding. Not that the message itself was in any way disturbing: It announced that he would arrive in Vienna on the morning of July 10 and provided more encouraging information about the bank. What troubled me was the name of the town from which the telegram had been sent: Bad Nauheim.

Bad Nauheim was best known as a place where cardiac cases went for treatment. I was thunderstruck. Could it be that Herzl was suffering from a heart condition? Impossible. To me, he had always been the very symbol of perfection—physical perfection as well as every other kind. I consulted a reference book and was relieved to find that Bad Nauheim was noted for the treatment of rheumatic and dermatological as well as cardiac disorders. Obviously, Herzl had gone there merely for a touch of rheumatism. If it had been anything serious, he would hardly be returning to Vienna so soon. Then, when he made his appearance at *Die Welt* on July 10, my last doubts were allayed. It was the old Herzl; he was in a good humor and accepted my congratulations on his London triumph with the familiar Herzl smile—that smile which seemed to betray just a hint of superiority to everything that was transpiring on this planet of ours.

Yet, just a few weeks earlier, Herzl had made an entry in his diary which told a very different story from that which I thought I read on his smiling face:

"Paris, June 19, at the Hotel Castille

"For sentiment's sake, I am staying again at the old house where four years ago I wrote *Der Judenstaat*. What a road I have traveled since then! And what weariness there has been. My heart is very fatigued. I suffer from constriction and arrhythmia."

Thus, the heart which had so long beat in sympathy with millions of oppressed Jews was now in a physical condition which would have aroused the sympathy and concern of all of us had we but known. I don't know whether I was insufficiently observant, whether I saw only what I wished to see, or whether it was Herzl who deliberately feigned perfect health. At all events, it never occurred to me that he was anything but his usual active, vigorous, robust self.

Herzl never uttered a word to suggest that he was in failing health or even that he was tired. I recall only two occasions on which he referred to his physical state at all. Once, he came into the office and remarked. "I have a terrific cold; it's got me positively groggy." Another time, he said good-humoredly, slowly moving his shoulders as though to test them: "I can hardly move today; I played tennis too long the day before yesterday." That was all—and yet we know now that he had far more to complain of than a bad cold and aching muscles.

Herzl wrote a *feuilleton* for the *Neue Freie Presse* dealing with his impressions of Bad Nauheim. Yet, it was difficult to say whether the author had been a patient (and, if so, what kind) or merely an observer who had chanced to pass through. I gladly seized upon the more optimistic interpretation, and before long the momentarily alarming telegram from Nauheim had completely vanished from my mind.

Rarely has a man spared himself as little in the service of a cause as Herzl did—while, at the same time, he spared his colleagues even the slightest disquiet by resolutely concealing the true state of his health.

*   *   *

Now a few words about Baroness Bertha von Suttner, whose name occurs at the beginning of this chapter. Born Countess Kinsky, a member of a Bohemian noble family, she was an ardent pacifist and president of the Austrian Society of Friends of Peace. In 1889, her novel, *Die Waffen nieder* ("Down Arms"), attracted wide attention. She was 56 years old at the time of The Hague Peace Conference. With her husband, Baron A. Gundaccar von Suttner, who was also a writer, she lived at Harmannsdorf castle near Eggenburg in Lower Austria.

As president of the Society for the Prevention of Anti-Semitism, Baron Suttner fought a brave though hopeless battle against the forces of organized bigotry in Austria. In an era when his only reward could be the scorn and abuse of his co-religionists, he and his wife spoke up publicly on behalf of the Jewish people. Both were contributors to *Die Welt*. Among my papers is a letter which Baroness Suttner wrote to Herzl on June 10, 1897, most of which was published in our third issue. In it, she said:

"The sample issue of *Die Welt* and all that you are doing inspires great respect in me. It shows courage, candor, clarity, a deep, firm will—with eyes fixed upon something great and useful.

"My feelings toward you and Zionism are like yours toward me and the peace movement: respect and doubt. One bids the boat 'God-speed'—but one cannot, *must* not go along, for on both sides the oarsmen must give no less than their all. I would have to study the matter before I could presume to say something about it. One can do harm, after all, by voicing doubts which stem from inadequate comprehension—in any case, only an accurate, qualified judgment is actually helpful."

Then Baroness Suttner made plain what her doubts were: "And I really don't know whether assimilation might not be better than founding a new state and nationality." It was typical of Herzl's tolerant approach that he published this non-Zionist view in *Die Welt*.

From this letter we learn what Herzl's attitude was toward pacifism and the striving for eternal peace: respect and doubt. Once in Reichenau, when we were discussing these matters, he said to me shaking his head: "It will be a long time before we see eternal peace, but the Jewish state will already be there—eternal." (The Reverend Hechler would probably have said: First must come the Kingdom of Israel, as prophesied; then the age of eternal peace will follow.)

Bertha von Suttner subsequently became a warm advocate of Zionism. In *Die Welt's* issue no. 21 for the year 1899, she expressed her feelings as follows: "As salvation from misery and persecution, as proud rebellion against unheard-of insults, and above all as the creation of a place of refuge—that is how I now see the establishment of the Kingdom of Zion."

In 1905, Baroness Suttner was awarded the Nobel Peace Prize. She died barely a month before the outbreak of

World War I. Thus, she did not live to see the tragic failure of her life's work, just as Herzl did not live to see the full fruition of his.

33

AMONG THE MEMORABILIA I have preserved from my days on *Die Welt* is a rather plain-looking post card, bearing a picture of the Wailing Wall in Jerusalem and several Oriental figures. Postmarked "Jerusalem 10/31/98," it is addressed to me and signed by Herzl and four others whose names were familiar to me: Josef Seidener, Dr. Schnirer, D. Wolffsohn and Dr. Bodenheimer.

Herzl and his collegues were in Jerusalem on a very special mission. They had gone there to greet Kaiser Wilhelm II of Germany, who was touring the Holy Land. Herzl hoped to induce the Kaiser to take the Zionist movement under his personal protection and help promote Jewish imigration to Palestine: a personal audience in Jerusalem, moreover, would have a tremendous impact on world opinion.

What I did not know when I received the post card was that, on the day it was written, Herzl was recovering from an attack of fever so severe that at one point his companions had despaired of his life. Nor did I know that he was racked by agonizing doubts: Would the Kaiser actually grant the audience which he had promised some weeks before? If not, the hoped-for triumph would be turned into a bitter defeat and a blow to the prestige of the entire Zionist movement.

At last, on November 2, the suspense was ended: Herzl was received by the Kaiser in Jerusalem. Here are excerpts from his account in issue no. 46 of *Die Welt* for 1898:

"An event has occurred in our movement whose importance requires no explanation. I refer to the audience granted the Zionist deputation in Jerusalem by the German Emperor.

"The audience was arranged at the beginning of October. In mid-October, the five-man deputation set out for Palestine . . .

"On November 2, the audience took place in the Emperor's tent at Jerusalem in the presence of Secretary of State [for Foreign Affairs] von Bülow. His Majesty the Emperor replied in most friendly fashion to the words addressed to him by Dr. Herzl . . .

"We did not go to Palestine as pleasure-seeking tourists or as explorers; we had a definite political purpose. When this had been accomplished, we immediately started home. Nevertheless, even during our brief stay we were able to make some observations and take note of conditions. Much of what we saw was dreary, but above the desolate, neglected countryside a glorious sky beamed down; and wherever a human hand had stirred, a bountiful Nature had cheerfully helped it to conjure forth swift abundance. The results achieved by our colonists, especially those who stand on their own feet, are simply astounding. All about, one still sees the stony, barren region into which one of these fine fellows plunged a few years before—he had coaxed an orange grove or a rich vineyard out of the soil . . .

"The Jewish farmers are tough and intelligent; that was our impression wherever we met them. Naturally, it was the picturesque details which struck us most vividly

on our hasty trip. Yet, conclusions can be drawn even from
these details. The colonists are, for example, good riders.
As we were arriving at Rehovoth, a troop of some twenty
young people came galloping up to escort us to the settlement. They performed a kind of Arab fantasia around
our carriages on their swift horses, and, watching these
sturdy, sunburnt lads whirl the horses around, dash off
into the fields and then ride shouting back, we could not
help thinking of the cowboys of the American Wild West.

"Unfortunately, we could visit only a few of the colonies, but we did get to know the Jewish farmer. He offers
great promise for the future.

"Yes, we still believe, and more than ever since we were
there, that this land which is so magnificently endowed
by Nature is a land of the future. This enchanting shore
by the blue sea can be turned into a Riviera by the civil-
izing force of large-scale colonization. To be sure, huge
investments are necessary; the country must be provided
with all the latest transportation and hygienic facilities.
But what scope it offers for the versatile, enterprising spirit
of a people that is thoroughly familiar with all modern
techniques, that has been raised in every civilized land.
And what a reward beckons at the end of these undertak-
ings. Large investments of labor and capital are necessary,
but labor bears golden fruits in this splendid clime and
capital, too, will bring a profit.

"On our hurried journey, we saw potentially fruitful
plains and beautiful mountains. Everywhere Nature is
waiting, conditions are waiting for the helping human
hand which should and can once more create gardens and
comfortable homes for men and women.

"Jerusalem made a powerful impression on us. Even
in its present decay one still sees the traces of former

beauty. And this city of many hills, which in some ways reminds one of Rome, could again become a magnificent metropolis. Looking down from the Mount of Olives, one can almost see the future city before one's eyes . . ."

Toward the end, Herzl's original manuscript refers to the fact that "we have succeeded in arousing the interest of a gifted monarch in our just cause." The German adjective preceding "monarch" is *"genial,"* which has the force of "genius-like" or "possessing genius." Before giving the manuscript to the printer, however, Herzl struck out "of a gifted *[genial]* monarch" and submitted the words "of two sovereigns." The original phrase, of course, was a reference to the Kaiser; the revised version was designed to include the Sultan of Turkey. The Sultan, who at that time ruled Palestine, had to be mentioned, but Herzl had no desire to refer to him as *"genial."* Hence the neutral formula, "of two sovereigns."

Wilhelm II was often described by his contemporaries as *"genial,"* since, unlike most other reigning monarchs of his day, he took a lively interest in the arts and sciences. Wilhelm Goldbaum, the pseudonymous "Spectator" who had once so enraged Dr. Eduard Glaser, lavished frequent tributes on him in the pages of *Die Welt* and once went so far as to hail his "sovereign genius." All this was with Herzl's full approval. The Kaiser seemed for a time very kindly disposed toward Zionism, and no compliments were spared in the effort to enlist his sympathy even further.

One day, I told Herzl that readers of *Die Welt* were complaining about the eulogies to the Kaiser. "Render unto the Kaiser what is the Kaiser's," he replied with a smile. When I reported further that my student friends were remarking that *Die Welt* "smeared too much honey on the Kaiser's mouth," Herzl was ready with another quip: "We should not be too stingy with honey when it is a question of winning the land that flows with milk and honey."

Whatever the precise extent of Herzl's admiration for the Kaiser, it was inevitably enhanced by the friendly, gracious manner in which the latter listened to his statement of the Zionist position. Herzl actually had two audiences with the German Emperor in the fall of 1898. The first took place on October 18 in Constantinople, where the Kaiser had paused briefly *en route* to Palestine. This was followed by the November 2 meeting in Jerusalem. On October 28, moreover, the Kaiser encountered Herzl at the Palestinian Jewish settlement of Mikveh Israel and stopped to exchange a few words. Herzl described the scene in his diary:

"Early yesterday morning, I rode out to Mikveh Israel...

"About 9, a movement on the highway, which was filled with a mixed multitude of Arab beggars, women, children and horsemen, heralded the approach of the Imperial train. Fierce Turkish horsemen galloped up at full tilt, with threatening weapons and even more threatening glances. Then came the Emperor's outriders. And finally, in a gray-clad group with several ladies, there was the Emperor himself.

"I gave the Mikveh student choir a signal to sing 'Hail to Thee in Victor's Wreath.' I stood at one of the plows and removed my cork helmet. The Emperor recognized me from a distance. He started slightly, directed his horse over to me, and stopped in front of me. I stepped forward two paces; when he bent down over the horse's neck and held out his hand to me, I stepped up close to his horse, extended my hand and stood before him with bared head.

"He laughed and his imperious eyes flashed at me:

" 'How are you?'

' 'Thank you, Your Majesty! I'm taking a look at the country. How has Your Majesty's trip been so far?'

"He blinked hard:

" 'Very hot! But the country has a future.'

" 'For the time being, it is still sick,' I said.

' 'It needs water, a great deal of water!' he replied.

" 'Yes, Your Majesty! Irrigation on a large scale!'

"He repeated: 'It is a land of the future'.

"He may have said something more which I have forgotten, for I stood there several minutes. Finally, he held out his hand to me again and trotted away. The Empress, who had also ridden out in front a bit, nodded to me smilingly. Then the Imperial train continued on its way amid the childish strains of 'Hail to Thee in Victor's Wreath.' . . .

"Among those riding along behind I recognized Lord Chamberlain Eulenburg, who greeted me pleasantly.

"The onlookers from Mikveh were utterly dumbfounded. Several asked who that was . . ."

The Reverend Hechler had played a considerable role in awakening interest in Herzl and winning him access to rulers like Wilhelm II. Hechler, who firmly believed that Herzl had been divinely appointed to lead the Jewish people back to the Promised Land, had dropped remarks at various German princely courts about a King of the Jews, a Messiah who was about to fulfill the ancient prophecies. Among the noble ladies in particular, this sort of romantic talk stirred intense curiosity. Was there really an uncrowned "King of the Jews," a new Moses who wanted to lead the Jews into the Promised Land? In his diary account of his audience with the Kaiser in Constantinople, Herzl tells of the following incident which occurred as he was climbing the stairs to the reception room:

"I was now standing at the top of the stairs. Count Kessel looked tensely over my shoulder; someone of note was evidently standing behind me on the portico. However, I did not turn around. Then we turned the corner, so that, glancing to the right, I could see who it was.

"A white dress—the Empress! She had been standing with Bülow behind a column and had seen me come up. I bowed; she made acknowledgement and disappeared."

Modesty prevented Herzl from making what would undoubtedly have been a more accurate statement: "She had been standing with Bülow behind a column in order to see me come up."

*   *   *

Influential persons at the German court, and to some extent the Kaiser himself, had encouraged Herzl to believe that Wilhelm II planned to sponsor the Jewish people's return to Palestine. For a time, indeed, the Kaiser actually did entertain the idea. Not that he was a great lover of the Jews. But the notion of assisting in the fulfilment of ancient prophecies, of proving himself the instrument of God's will and taking a great historic event under his personal aegis, was one that appealed to him.

In those days, monarch like Wilhelm II could still exercise a powerful influence on the course of history, and a private individual like Herzl who hoped to make history was compelled to court their favor. Herzl's natural diplomatic gifts fitted him admirably for his task. He knew how to preserve his personal dignity in dealing with the mighty of this earth, how to show himself their equal and yet avoid unseemly familiarity. It was as though an inner voice said to him: "You stand here as the spokesman of an ancient people, one which has been called 'the People of God'; show that you are worthy of playing this role."

For all of us at *Die Welt,* the days which followed Herzl's return from Palestine were filled with tense anticipation of great events. Herzl himself was convinced that the Ingathering of the Exiles was indeed at hand after 2,000 years. He made no public statement, but among friends he freely voiced his glowing hopes. The fact that the Kaiser had as yet given no official sign of his intentions did not disturb Herzl. The mills of emperors, like those of gods, grind slowly.

Herzl could already see gaily beflagged ships, crowded with joyful Jewish families, weighing anchor in Mediterranean and other ports and setting out toward the east. I remember him spreading out a map of Palestine on his desk and debating whether the harbor at Jaffa or at Haifa was better suited to receive the immigrants. He had observed conditions at Jaffa on his recent trip, and, though he had never been to Haifa, he had obtained detailed information about its harbor. As he tapped here and there on the map with his pencil, the rest of us stood and listened, caught in the spell of his enthusiasm.

Herzl loved to let his imagination dwell on the immigrant ship with its happy human cargo. But his dreams were more ambitious yet. He foresaw ultimately a whole fleet of ships, manned entirely by Jews and sailing from Jewish ports under the Jewish flag, which would bring the dispersed children of Israel back to the land of their fathers. Once, he remarked to me: "Don't forget that our nearest neighbors to the north in ancient times were the Phoenicians, a race of stout-hearted seafarers."

Before long, however, sober reality intruded upon Herzl's exuberant dreams of the future. The Kaiser's failure to proclaim his official sponsorship of the Zionist movement could no longer be overlooked; he had obviously decided not to support the Jewish return to Palestine. All our soaring hopes came fluttering down to earth.

It was one of the most difficult periods in Herzl's life. Yet, like a commander who feels responsible for upholding his men's morale, he was able to conceal from us to some extent the bitter disappointment that he felt. Herzl was not one to be crushed by a defeat, to be laid permanently low by a cruel blow of fate. He had, as it were, the spiritual elasticity of his people, whom history had taught that life is largely a series of unpredictable ups and downs.

Herzl also inclined to the philosophical attitude that "all is for the best." "In our failure there is also a success," he said to me regarding the German fiasco. "They are obviously taking us seriously. The times are past when they used to laugh at us. Zionism is taken so seriously that the statesmen are afraid we might endanger international relations. We are no longer ridiculous; we are dangerous." In a subsequent conversation, he remarked: "Patience! Many roads lead to Jerusalem; they don't necessarily have to pass through Potsdam." And he added with some bitterness: "*Raison d'état* prevents the Kaiser from extending his protection to us. Again it's that . . . *raison d'état*." (The modifier preceding *raison d'état* was one of those generally rendered as "blankety-blank.")

Despite his disappointment, Herzl recognized some of the factors which might explain and even excuse the Kaiser's behavior. The other powers, especially Russia, might become suspicious if Germany established a Jewish protectorate in the Near East. There was also the delicate question of German relations with Turkey, whose Sultan was suzerain of Palestine. We were gratefully aware that the Kaiser had attempted to raise the issue of Zionism in several conversations with the Sultan, but each time Abdul Hamid had made it plain that the subject was distasteful to him. It was scarcely surprising that, faced with the choice of displeasing either the Sultan of Turkey or Theodor Herzl, the Kaiser had taken the latter course—particularly since many of his advisers and courtiers were anything but sympathetic to Zionism. Whatever his irritation at the dictates of *raison d'état,* Herzl bore the Kaiser himself no ill will. He was grateful for the latter's original good intentions, for the efforts he had made, and particularly for the personal sympathy he had shown Herzl at their meetings.

When it became apparent that the Kaiser was no longer inclined to come forward as sponsor of the Jewish return to Palestine, Herzl made a last attempt to revive his flagging interest. He felt it his duty to the Jewish people not to let this unique opportunity slip from his grasp without a struggle. As soon as he saw that it was hopeless, however, he wrote the Kaiser off as a prospect and the name Wilhelm II vanished from our conversational repertoire. Herzl never lingered on his way to bemoan a disappointed hope. He could adapt himself to the fact that what at first seemed the dawn of an era had proved merely a passing episode. Time would bring new opportunities.

Was Herzl guilty of guillible stargazing in this whole affair? On the contrary, only an arch-skeptic could have dismissed the impressive evidence pointing to success. On October 7, even before his audiences with the Kaiser, Herzl had visited the latter's close confidant, Count Philip

Eulenburg, at Liebenberg Castle. There Eulenburg told him that the Kaiser was very sympathetic toward Zionism and had fully accepted the idea of establishing a German "protectorate" over the Zionist movement. The Kaiser was also confident that he could obtain the Sultan's approval of large-scale Jewish settlement in Palestine. In addition, Eulenburg said he had won the influential support of German Foreign Secretary Bernhard von Bülow for Herzl's plans. When all this was followed by the Kaiser's display of keen personal interest at Constantinople and Jerusalem, Herzl could scarcely be blamed for thinking that his hopes and dreams were on the verge of fulfilment.

34

WHILE *EN ROUTE* from Constantinople to Palestine for his second audience with the Kaiser, Herzl had made a stop at the Egyptian port city of Alexandria. A letter which he wrote from Alexandria to Dr. Sieg-mund Werner, then Executive Editor of *Die Welt*, clearly showed the high hopes with which he had undertaken the journey:

"Alexandria harbor, October 24,1898
"Dear Doctor,

"Just a few words in great haste. You will soon learn all the facts about our expedition, which had to be kept a secret. For the time being, I can only tell you that a manuscript of some importance may arrive from Pales-tine for publication in *Die Welt*. The day it is mailed, I will send you a wire, 'Manuscript dispatched,' whereupon

you should arrange to give it the top position in the next
issue after its arrival . . .

"In any case, reserve all the best articles you have for
that issue. Perhaps you will get a good *feuilleton* soon
from L. Kellner, as well as a good 'Week' column from
Erwin and a good 'World Chronicle.' I will also wire you
about the size of the press-run."

In the letter, Herzl used the words "sensational" and
"gala" in referring to the issue which was to contain his
report from Palestine. Yet, he did no more than hint
mysteriously at the subject of the forthcoming report.

Herzl was sometimes accused of deliberate "secret-mon-
gering," since he rarely spoke about his future plans on
behalf of Zionism and even drew the veil of secrecy over
many things which he had already accomplished. The
fact is, however, that he had excellent reasons for acting
this way. If he gained a reputation for lack of discretion,
he would lose the ear of the influential figures in various
countries whose favor was so vitally important. Moreover,
by blurting out the details of a project which was still in
mid-course, he would risk giving his enemies the means
to block its successful completion. Herzl's journalistic
background was also a factor here. As a newspaperman, he
had long since acquired the habit of jealously guarding a
piece of newsworthy information until the moment when
it was to be made public.

The care Herzl took to preserve his negotiations with
the Kaiser from premature publicity is shown in a postscript to his Alexandria letter to Dr. Werner:

"Naturally, apart from my papa, the Colonel [von Eiss,
then business manager of *Die Welt*] and Rosenberger,
no one is to know about this beforehand. Also, keep the

manuscript at the printer's, so that no one sees it in advance.

"I will send the manuscript special delivery to Bergman's printshop under your name. It will come by way of Brindisi. On the day it is due, you will have to stay at the printer's around the clock.

"Kindest regards to our dear Colonel and our doughty Erwin, and also to you, from all my traveling companions!

"It will probably be the second issue in November, that is, November 11."

35

OF THE REGULAR FEATURES in *Die Welt,* Herzl's favorite was unquestionably the column we called "The Week." In the first issue, "The Week" came immediately after the new magazine's "Program" and the lead article, both of which Herzl himself had written. In subsequent issues, it invariably held the second spot following the lead article.

"The Week" consisted of a series of short paragraphs (*"G'setzln"* in our Viennese German), separated by three stars, which offered comment on current news. Another column, "World Chronicle," listed events in a straightforward, factual manner, leaving the interpretation to "The Week."

From the very start, "The Week" was characterized by a strong note of satire—a quality which was prominent in most of Herzl's writing. "The Week" was the most outspoken, subjective feature of *Die Welt*—its ego, one might almost say—and the weapon of satire came naturally to hand in the magazine's never-ending two-front war: against its adversaries within the Jewish camp and against the far more menacing foe of anti-Semitism.

At this point, a word of warning is in order. There has been a tendency among scholars to credit Herzl with the authorship of all or nearly all the unsigned "Week" columns. This is a serious error. It is true that many of these columns were in fact a product of Herzl's pen, but it is equally true that many of them were not. It is quite erroneous to assume that any "Week" which seems to bear some of the characteristic marks of Herzl's style can safely be included in his collected works. The only articles and columns which should be attributed to him are those which he signed or whose authenticity is attested either by a reliable witness or by the existence of the original manuscript.

The very first "Week" column, in issue no. 1 of *Die Welt,* serves to illustrate this point. It was a veritable literary *pot pourri,* with various paragraphs written by Herzl, S. R. Landau and myself and edited by Herzl. Nor was this the only such mixed offering.

After he had written a number of entire columns himself, though without signature, the press of work forced Herzl to give up contributing to "The Week" altogether. It was accordingly turned over to Felix Salten, the Viennese writer and editor.* Since Salten did not wish to be publicly identified with the column, it continued to appear anonymously.

Then, one morning, Herzl said to me with a friendly smile and a note of gentle teasing combined with seriousness: "Rosenberger, I believe you are now called to higher things."

*Felix Salten was later to become world-famous as the author of *Bambi.*

After a pause, he cleared up the mystery: "Would you like to take over 'The Week'?"

I could only echo in astonishment: " 'The Week'?"

"Yes, our column 'The Week.' I would like it to be *your* column, to be written entirely by you from now on."

I said I would be delighted to take the assignment. Then Herzl paid me a few compliments: He said he was certain the column would be in good hands; he needed to give me no special instructions, since I was thoroughly familiar with "The Week"'s requirements. And besides, he added, he would always be there to see that I committed no grave indiscretions.

Needless to say, I noticed the slight contradiction between the last remark and the preceding assurance of confidence. However, while I might have resented the supervision of another man, I was only too happy to have Herzl as the guardian angel who guided my footsteps past possible pitfalls. If he, in his superior wisdom, should decide to delete part or all of some future "Week" column which I had produced, then so be it. And, indeed, more than a few of my *G'setzln*—and, once or twice, complete columns —were consigned to the waste-paper basket in order to avoid unpleasant repercussions.

*   *   *

One day toward the end of March 1900, our office boy brought me some proofs from Herzl's home, together with the following letter from I. Schalit:

"Dear Rosenberger:

"Dr. Herzl asks me to tell you that your 'Week' column, although it is very good, must *under no circumstances* be published. It cannot even be rewritten. You will have to leave 'The Week' out altogether this time and run more

'World Chronicle' (or perhaps an appropriate article) in its place.

Regards,
SCHALIT"

Although we had been just about to go to press, the problem was solved without too much difficulty. The gap left by the disappearance of "The Week"—comprising all of page 8 and part of 9—I filled with material for our "Periodical Review" column from the overset. I also inserted a note on page 9: "Due to a technical error, the 'Week' column had to be left out this time at the last moment."

Nevertheless, as I had the type for "The Week" removed from the form, I could not help wondering what had prompted Herzl to order such a radical operation. Why could the column "under no circumstances" be printed, even though it was "very good"? I glanced through the proofs once more in the hope of finding a clue. There was a reference to the recently approved electoral reform, which seemed likely to assure indefinite control of the Vienna Municipal Council by its anti-Semitic majority. Surely this was not the offending item. The column then went on to tell of the hearing granted a delegation of Jewish citizens by Austrian Prime Minister Koerber. The group's spokesman, Reichsrat Deputy Auspitz, had reported to the Prime Minister on conditions among Austrian Jews and had received assurances of good treatment for his co-religionists. "The Week" commented editorially on the glaring contrast between the harsh blows dealt the Jews by the Vienna electoral reform and the meager balm afforded by Koerber. It suggested that the Prime Minister, who had surely played a part in approving the electoral reform, might have granted his gracious audience at precisely this time in a calculated move to sugarcoat the bitter pill which the Jews were being forced to swallow.

None of this seemed at the time to provide an explanation for Herzl's peremptory veto. Not until two decades later, with the publication of Herzl's *Diaries,* was the mystery solved. During this period, Prime Minister Koerber had several times invited Herzl to the Interior Ministry for a friendly private discussion of Austrian domestic politics. Koerber had not been courting the favor of Herzl the Zionist but of Herzl the editor of the *Neue Freie Presse.* At that time, it was commonly said in Austria: "No government can rule against the opposition of the *Neue Freie Presse.*" Hence, the Prime Minister had privately asked Herzl to prevail upon the publishers of the powerful journal to temper their editorial attacks on the approval of the electoral reform and on Koerber personally. The latter had insisted that he was helpless to oppose the anti-Semites on this issue. Eager to maintain good relations with the Prime Minister for the sake of the Zionist movement and the new Jewish bank, Herzl had acceded to his request; the anticipated onslaught on Koerber in the *Presse* failed to materialize. In the light of these facts, about which none of us at *Die Welt* had known at the time, everything became clear. Had my "Week" column been permitted to run in the issue of March 28, 1900, after the understanding Herzl had reached with Koerber, the latter would have had every reason to accuse Herzl of playing a double game.

36

ON MAY 1, 1899, Dr. Siegmund Werner left *Die Welt* to devote himself completely to his medical practice. The announcement in the magazine closed with the sentence: "The position of Executive Editor is being taken over by Mr. Edwin Rosenberger, who, as our readers are aware, has belonged to the staff of our paper since the first issue." Remembering how blissfully ignorant of everything pertaining to journalism I had been two short years before when I joined *Die Welt,* I felt that Herzl had indeed honored me.

The post of Executive Editor (or "Responsible Editor," to give the literal translation of this Central European journalistic title) was not the same on our magazine as on some others. On many publications, he was merely a "straw man" without the slightest influence on policy. Often, in fact, he was not even a member of the editorial staff but rather a printer or other outsider who—generally for money—agreed to assume legal responsibility for the contents of the paper and to bear any penalties it might incur for violating the law. The result sometimes was that a "Responsible Editor" went to jail for an article he had never read, let alone written. His function was, quite simply, that of a scapegoat or whipping boy.

It was different on *Die Welt.* As "Responsible Editor" I was, to be sure, legally responsible for the contents of the magazine. However, I knew those contents intimately; part I wrote myself, and the rest I helped select and edited. I also had the right to object to an article about which I had reservations. Nevertheless, my occasional disagreements with Herzl in such matters never reached the point of a serious clash. He was always willing to give due consideration to any reasonable argument, and for my part I was eager to fulfill his editorial desires. I often held my peace about an article which I knew was important to him, even when, as the "responsible" member of the staff, I might have had good reason to remonstrate. I don't believe it is an exaggeration to say that I would willingly have gone to jail if it had meant rendering Herzl some special service.

In elevating me to my new dignity, Herzl had no fear that I would prove unequal to the editorial and technical demands of the job. Only one thing gave him concern: the possible excesses of what he referred to as my "temperament." By that he meant my tendency to combativeness, which was not always accompanied by an equal measure of prudence. So long as he was in Vienna, he could keep a checkrein on me; he no longer read the galley proofs as in the first weeks of the magazine, but he did read the page proofs and thus could still remove any potentially dangerous material before the presses actually started rolling. However, Herzl was not always in Vienna. His various journeys on behalf of Zionism, as well as his vacations, left *Die Welt* unprotected against my outbreaks of "temperament."

Some years later, I discovered in the *Herzl Yearbook* edited by Tulo Nussenblatt the following interesting letter which Herzl had written to Dr. Werner shortly after I assumed my new duties:

"Vienna, June 5, 1899
"Dear Friend:
"I must go away for several weeks and have a request to make of you. Will you read through the pages each

Wednesday—don't correct them, but merely make a final check to see that there are no indiscretions. I have absolute confidence in our friend Rosenberger, of course, but he is young and temperamental. Two pairs of eyes see more, and you, after all, know the special tone of *Die Welt*, if I may say so.

"I would be very grateful for an immediate answer.

"Sincerely yours,
HERZL"

What Werner's reply was I cannot say, but I do know that he never approached me with an offer to give the proofs a "final check." We had always gotten on well together, and he must have turned down Herzl's suggestion rather than create ill will between us. Flushed as I was with newly acquired power, I would unquestionably have rejected any overtures from Werner with great indignation.

37

THERE WERE MANY PEOPLE who regarded Herzl as the Messiah, the Anointed of the Lord who would fulfill the ancient prophecies and bring salvation. This view was even shared by some non-Jews, one of whom, as we have seen, was the Reverend Hechler, chaplain of the British Embassy in Vienna.

I still have many of the letters of love and veneration which Herzl used to receive from his followers in every part of the world. One, for example, is from Salomon Farb of Focsani, Rumania. In faulty German but with an impressive display of Biblical learning, the writer concludes from various words and numbers in the Old Testament that the Messianic era is approaching. "The Messiah," he adds, "may now be Theodor Herzl, the Anointed of the Lord."

In another letter, which reached Herzl after the First Zionist Congress, Rabbi N. Benjamin writes from the United States on behalf of a group of singers: "Everywhere the name of Dr. Herzl is worshiped like that of a deity . . . *You* are the divine emissary to whom was given the mission of once again raising up Jerusalem and the cities of Judah, as the prophets promised . . . In New York, Brooklyn, Philadelphia, Boston, Baltimore, Chicago, the idea is meeting with a great response among Jews of all religious shades."

If genealogy has any bearing in such matters, then Herzl's origin may be said to have been one that would befit a Messiah. He was descended from the tribe of Levi, of which Moses was also a scion. His ancestors were the Levites, who for centuries, as priests and servants of priests, had guarded the holy places of Israel. In a letter of December 9, 1898, addressed to Jonas Wolpe, he wrote:

"Dear Sir!

"Forgive me for being so late in replying to your kind letter, but I am very much overburdened with correspondence. My good father Jacob Herzl is ben Shimon Halevi. The Hebrew name of my good mother Jeanette Herzl is Channe bath Gabriel Harsch.

With Zionist greetings, sincerely yours,
DR. HERZL"

As I have already mentioned in an earlier chapter, Herzl was not averse to popularity, since a rise in his personal popularity inevitably redounded to the advantage of the movement he headed. He did not actively pursue popularity, however, nor did he need it. And, when it came, he did not brush it aside with a show of false modesty. Yet, when praise went beyond all bounds and degenerated into sycophancy, he reacted vigorously. On one such occasion, I received the following letter from him:

"Vienna, October 19 [1899]
"Dear friend,
   "On page 6, in the article 'Zionism in Hungary,' the grotesque adulatory passage about me in the second column must *absolutely be taken out.* After all, I cannot allow myself to be made ridiculous.
                              "Cordially yours,
                                        H."

I hastened to remove the offending passage, which, as it happened, was not in an original article written for *Die Welt* but in a report which we were reprinting from the *Ungarische Wochenschrift.* Hungary was a kind of Eldorado for the Jews in those days, and the Hungarian Jews showed little enthusiasm for the idea of a Jewish state. Hence, we regarded any sign of change in attitude as a fact worth noting.

The Hungarian Jews sought in various ways to show their gratitude for the friendly treatment they received from their Magyar neighbors. They did their best to assimilate, and many of them "Magyarized" their German names. In fact, Herzl had a nephew, a Hungarian author and dramatist, who went by the name of "Heltai."

*   *   *

Occasionally, I took a hand at writing lead articles for *Die Welt.* One day in May 1900, Herzl said to me in an almost fierce tone: "Rosenberger, draw your broad battle sword and smite the Mainz *Israelit!*"

The *Israelit* was an orthodox Jewish paper, published in the German city of Mainz, which had earned our cordial dislike for the disagreeable manner in which it combated Zionism. Herzl did not have to tell me twice to "smite" the *Israelit;* I dipped my "broad battle sword" in the ink-well and laid about me with great gusto. When I sent the proofs of the article to Herzl's home for approval, I had no doubt that it contained a sufficient amount of "smiting." Unfortunately, it contained too much. The proofs came back with the following note:

"Vienna, May 10, 1900

"Dear friend,

"Unless you take out the passages I have marked for deletion, you'll have a bad lawsuit on your hands.

"Cordially yours,

TH. H."

Even in its modified form, the article met with the disapproval of many of our readers who sympathized with the *Israelit's* orthodox religious position. However, I could console myself with the thought that I had been a good soldier and carried out my commander's orders.

38

THE YEAR 1899 WAS, among other things, a ritual-murder year. To many readers of this book, the words "ritual murder" may mean little or nothing. To the Jews of medieval Europe, however, and to the Jews of

Central and Eastern Europe as recently as the early years of this century, they conjured up a nightmarish picture of superstitious hatred and irrational violence.

Many centuries ago, some sick mind concocted the fable that the Jews made a practice of murdering Christians in order to use their blood in religious rituals. A favorite version was that the blood was used to season matzoth during the Jewish Passover festival. Orthodox Jews were said to be the prime offenders.

Had the propagators of the ritual-murder myth been open to reasonable argument, it would have been a simple matter to convince them that the very tenets of the Jewish religion forbade such practices. Thus, Chapter 17 of the Book of Leviticus contains God's warning:

"And whatsover man there be of the house of Israel, or of the strangers that sojourn among them, that eateth any manner of blood, I will set my face against that soul that eateth blood, and will cut him off from among his people."

And a little further on we find the dietary law "Therefore I said unto the children of Israel, No soul of you shall eat blood, neither shall any stranger that sojuorneth among you eat blood."

And then a third time: "Therefore I said unto the children of Israel, Ye shall eat the blood of no manner of flesh; for the life of all flesh is the blood thereof: whosoever eateth it shall be cut off."

Quotations from the Old Testament, however, made little impression on those blinded by malice or ignorance. Often, it took no more than one mischief-seeking idler or simple-minded yokel to insure that an otherwise uneventful year would go down in the Jews' private annals of sorrow as a "ritual-murder year." And, once the fatal cry had been raised, not only the alleged murderer but every Jew in the vicinity was certain to feel the fury of the mob.

On March 29, 1899, the body of a murder victim was found in the woods near the little Bohemian town of Polna; it proved to be that of a 19-year-old seamstress, Agnes Hruza, of nearby Klein-Weznitz. Before long, the word was passing from mouth to mouth among the villagers: The Jews did it—ritual murder! All that remained was to find the Jewish murderer. The choice quickly fell on a local cobbler named Leopold Hülsner (or Hilsner), a harmless, somewhat feeble-minded individual who, ironically enough, was the son of a Christian father and a Jewish mother.

Branded by people, Hülsner was turned over to the authorities. He was subjected to a thoroughgoing examination by the local magistrate, Reichenbach, a conscientious official deaf to the clamor in the streets, who quickly realized that the guileless cobbler knew nothing whatever about the murder and ordered him released. The mob would not stand for this, however, and the intimidated town officials took Hülsner back into custody. As an anti-Semitic-Deputy in the Austrian Parliament candidly expressed it: "Only when the population assumed a threatening attitude was Hülsner finally arrested." What happened next was described in the *Wiener Tagblatt* of April 13:

"The following evening, the street-rabble of Polna gathered at three places in the town and, with shouts of 'The Jews murdered the Hruza girl! Let's go after the Jews! Down with the Jews!', marched into the Jewish quarter, which contains forty families. At the Karlsplatz, where the Jewish temple and the community center are located, the stoning of Jewish houses began. The attacks were directed against the Schiller tannery, the home of tavern-keeper Simon Furcht and the grain merchant Emanuel Basch.

A crowd of perhaps 300 people of the town's better classes looked on in silence at these brutal scenes. A local policeman and two constables—all that the security organs could muster—were powerless to prevent the outrages."

Order was finally restored by a police inspector and twelve constables who were sent over from nearby Deutsch-Brod. In the meantime, news of the events in Polna had been received with great rejoicing in anti-Semitic political circles in Vienna. The Jew-baiting press promptly sent reporters to the scene—talented individuals who conducted private investigations of the "ritual murder" and did their best to stoke the flames of anti-Semitic fury in Bohemia, while at the same time they sent back inflammatory dispatches for the edification of readers in Vienna and the provinces. One of the worst offenders in the campaign of incitement was the Vienna *Deutsches Volksblatt,* an organ of the Christian Social party which basked in the special favor of the Viennese municipal authorities.

It was in this poisoned atmosphere that Leopold Hülsner was brought to trial in the district court of Kuttenberg in Bohemia. Judges and jurymen alike were influenced by the force of "public opinion," the endless "ritual murder" refrain in the streets, the sense of impending violence. Under the circumstances, the outcome was foreordained. The twelve members of the jury brought in a verdict of "Guilty!" and on September 16, after a trial lasting five days, the court pronounced sentence: Death by hanging.

The scene in the courtroom during the trial was described by the *Neue Freie Presse:*

"In the spectators' section of the courtroom, just as outside, one continually heard people saying, with the greatest assurance and in a vehement tone, that the accused had done the deed and that he had done it out of religious motives. The spectators in the room engaged in frequent and loud demonstrations of a kind that would never have been possible in a Vienna courtroom. They treated the accused and his lawyer to rebuttals, muttering, mockery and laughter; they applauded the prosecution witnesses; they repeatedly gave vent to an ironic 'Oho!' during the presentation of evidence, when mention was made of the Polna examining magistrate, who was known to have had doubts about Hülsner's guilt. Several anti-Semitic Czech journalists were the leaders of the chorus; one of them, a man with rolling eyes, gave signals with a crutch which he had lying next to him. When several Viennese journalists mildly remonstrated that their work was being disturbed, they were greeted with abuse—though only, it is true, by their anti-Semitic colleagues. The calls to order which the bench addressed to the spectators from time to time were heeded for only a few minutes. Hülsner had as yet only been accused, but he had also been condemned already in advance. The questions put to him by the prosecutor, by the jurymen and even by the presiding judge showed clearly that all of them were convinced not only of his crime but also of the ritual murder. The word ['*Ritualmord*'] was not uttered by them, nor even by the court medical experts . . . It was like a party game in which no one is allowed to say a certain word, with the result that everyone thinks of it all the more."

Despite his conviction, however, Hülsner was not destined to be hanged just yet. His undaunted defense counsel, Dr. Zdenko Aurednizek, entered a plea of nullity, thereby blocking execution of the sentence at least temporarily. Sincerely convinced of his client's innocence, Aurednizek had defended him with all his heart and soul, braving the insults of the mob and the savage gibes of the prosecutor, an anti-Semitic Czech Deputy in Parliament.

In the two days which followed Hülsner's sentencing, two telegrams, one from Russia and one from Upper Austria, arrived in the office of *Die Welt*. The first, which came from St. Petersburg, had obviously been written in great agitation; a reply had been paid for in advance. The sender was Dr. Brutzkos, Secretary of the Russian Jewish weekly *Voskhod*, who reported that the anti-Semitic Russian newspaper *Novoye Vremya* had just published an alarming dispatch from Vienna on the Kuttenberg trial. From the samples he gave, it was apparent that the *Novoye Vremya's* report was a typical atrocity story, filled with distortions of the kind at which the *Deutsches Volksblatt* excelled. The telegram concluded: "Editors *Voskhod* urgently request you wire at once setting facts straight. . . ." Dr. Brutzkus was obviously concerned with making the truth known without delay before the anti-Semitic outbreak in Bohemia spread to Russia. I promptly sent him a factual account of what had happened.

The second telegram had been sent from the Austrian resort town of Unterach. It read: "Other than Erter's article please run only purely objective report on Polna. Am coming Thursday. Herzl."

Newspaper criticism of a judicial decision was a punishable offense under Austrian law, and Herzl feared I might be carried away by my understandable indignation at the Hülsner verdict. The report which I then proceeded to write cannot be said to have been "purely objective," for I minced no words about the anti-Semitic atmosphere in the courtroom and the pitifully inadequate evidence. However, I took care not to criticize the august gentlemen on the bench, and Herzl passed my article. (The "Erter" referred to in Herzl's telegram, incidentally, was Dr. Wilhelm Goldbaum, who used a variety of pseudonyms in writing for *Die Welt*. Twenty-three years older than Herzl and an experienced journalist, Goldbaum could be safely relied upon to keep his comments well within the bounds of legality.)

The next few weeks were marked by anti-Semitic outbreaks in many parts of the Czech provinces of Bohemia and Moravia, which drove thousands of Jews from their homes. On Thursday, October 5, in the midst of these events, Herzl walked into our print-shop on the *Schlösselgasse* shortly before the latest issue was to go to press. I could see at once that he had something important to say. "Hülsner has been proved innocent," he announced without further ado. "The real murderer has been apprehended and has already confessed." Then he added, with a look of deep disgust on his face: "The whole filthy Polna affair is over."

Though we had all expected Hülsner to be vindicated eventually, this sudden news surprised me. Herzl offered no hint as to where he had obtained the information, but his confident tone indicated that it had been a reliable source. He handed me a sheet of paper containing a brief announcement, which I promptly took into the composing room. When *Die Welt* came out the next day, the following paragraph appeared in bold type in the "World Chronicle" column:

"According to information reaching us from a trustworthy source just before we go to press, the Polna affair is about to take a sensational turn. If our informant's facts are correct, Hülsner's innocence may be conclusively demonstrated in the next few days. Suspicion of responsibility for the murder has in recent days been directed toward a lead which was pursued at the beginning but later dropped. At the moment, we are not in a position to go into further detail."

Unfortunately, however, these hopeful lines were not borne out by events. The "sensational turn" predicted by "a trustworthy source" did not come about.

* * *

The Polna case affected Herzl much as it did the rest of us: It left him indignant yet resigned. He was indignant at the "ritual murder" slander and its contemptible perpetrators. Yet, he accepted such periodic explosions of anti-Semitic frenzy in a resigned mood as facts of life that had to be faced; it was obviously useless to try to purge this darkness from men's souls.

None of us ruled out the possibility that Hülsner had actually, for some reason, committed the murder; if so, we were perfectly content to see justice take its course. What embittered us was the fact that, quite apart from the question of guilt or innocence, the case was being used to perpetuate a fantastic medieval myth about the Jewish people. For my part, as I groped through the tangled mass of information about the trial, I could not find a shred of what appeared to be real evidence against the accused, and I gradually came to the conclusion that Hülsner had had nothing to do with the murder.

To their eternal credit, a number of non-Jews raised their voices against the shameful events of Bohemia. One of them was a distinguished professor at the Czech University in Prague, who conducted a private investigation at Polna and then published a pamphlet in which he pointed out various glaring contradictions in the case against Hülsner, demolished the theory that a "ritual murder" had been comitted, and flatly demanded a review of the trial. His name was Thomas G. Masaryk; nineteen years later, he was to be the founder and first President of the Czechoslovak Repulic. Herzl commented to me at

the time: "Men like Professor Masaryk and Public Prosecutor Bobies, not to mention the Emperor, restore a little
of one's faith that the decent, sane people have not died
out yet."

Emperor Franz Joseph of Austria-Hungary had just
made a forthright gesture of sympathy to his Jewish subjects by bestowing a high honor on the Rabbi of Prague.
The latter's reception at the Imperial Palace was described as follows in a published account:

"One of those whom the Emperor received in the general audiences at the Vienna *Hofburg* on the morning of
December 11 was the Rabbi of the Jewish religious community of Prague, Dr. Alexander Kisch. Dr. Kisch had
come to express gatitude to the monarch for awarding
him the golden Distinguished Service Cross with Crown.
When the Rabbi, who was clad in his religious robes,
entered the audience chamber, he requested the Emperor's
permission to cover his head and say the prayer prescribed
by the Mosaic religion. The Emperor granted permission,
and the Rabbi, first in German and then in Hebrew, uttered the words: 'May the reflected splendor and richest
blessings of divine majesty ever rest on Your Majesty's
head.' The Emperor thanked him, and Dr. Kisch expressed
his gratitude for the decoration, to which the monarch
replied: 'I was very pleased to decorate you, for I know
your loyalty and your services. . . .' Dr. Kisch then said:
'My co-religionists in my more immediate fatherland of
Bohemia feel this gratitude with me in these difficult days,
for the favor of Your Majesty is their only comfort.' The
Emperor thereupon replied: 'Yes, your co-religionists are
passing through difficult days now, but things have already
become better.' 'Yes, they are passing through difficult
days, Your Majesty,' said Dr. Kisch, and the Emperor continued: 'I am very indignant at these brutal acts.' The

monarch then repeated the word: 'at this brutality.' Dr.
Kisch requested permission to inform his co-religionists
of these gracious words, and the Emperor said to him:
'Please do so.' With that the audience ended."

Public Prosecutor Bobies had taken legal action against
the anti-Semitic *Deutsches Volksblatt* for its exploitation
of the Hülsner case. The following excerpt is from a report
of the proceedings:

"In his presentation, the Public Prosecutor, Dr. Bobies,
described the aforementioned newspaper's attitude in the
Polna affair, which it had exploited for purely political
purposes. No sooner had a few witnesses been heard than
it had pronounced Hülsner the guilty party and expressed
the sure conviction that ritual murder was involved. The
paper had needed a ritual murder for its reading public,
and it had used a crime committed by one individual to
make a terrible accusation against the entire Jewish people.
. . . We had all heard of the splendid Legal Committee
which had been formed at the instance of the *Deutsches
Volksblatt* and had had no other purpose than to mislead
the public and create a sensation for the paper's readers."

The "Responsible Editor" of the *Volksblatt* was found
guilty and sentenced to a term in jail. Dr. Carl Bobies, who
had prosecuted him, was widely known for his unbending
devotion to justice. A sturdy, blond-haired man whose
shrewd gray eyes looked out from behind gold-rimmed
spectacles, he had been outraged by the anti-Semitic fabri-
cations and intrigue which marked the Hülsner case.
Needless to say, he was bitterly hated by the members of
the anti-Semitic bloc in Parliament, who took advantage
of their immunity to shower him with abuse for moving
against the *Volksblatt*. Yet, he proceeded with a second
action—this time against the Editor of the equally anti-
Semitic *Ostdeutsche Rundschau*. Once again, a primary

count in the accusation was the paper's use of the ritual-murder slander, and once again the defendant was found guilty.

*   *   *

In the meantime, the fate of Leopold Hülsner hung in the balance. His lawyer's appeal against the Kuttenberg verdict had stressed the denial of a number of defense motions during the trial, including a motion to produce in court a vagabond named Franz Wehr who had been arrested in the Bohemian town of Warnsdorf for murder and a moral offense. Weeks and months passed while the Austrian Supreme Court studied the appeal and the trial record.

All the while, the condemned man himself awaited the outcome with utter indifference. His limited faculties were no more capable of grasping the full significance of the sentence than they had been of understanding the original charge. It would probably have meant little more to him if he had been accused of complicity in the murder of Julius Caesar.

At last, in early May 1900, Hülsner was brought before the president of the Kuttenberg district court and informed that the Supreme Court had unanimously set aside the death sentence. He was to be held for retrial in another locality. The prisoner received the news without the slightest show of interest.

The new trial was set for July 12 in the district court of Pisek, another small Bohemian town. There was obviously no reason to suppose that the twelve jurors to be selected from the townspeople of Pisek would prove any more enlightened than their compatriots in Kuttenberg. At the end of June, it was announced that the trial had been postponed until the fall to give the judges an opportunity to sift through the huge mass of material that had accumulated around the unfortunate cobbler. The additional time was precisely what the anti-Semites needed to set the stage effectively. Before long, the agitators who had done their work so well in Polna and Kuttenberg were arriving in force in Pisek and the region was flooded with leaflets depicting the horrors of ritual murder and inciting the populace against the Jews. At the same time, the anti-Semitic Czech Deputy whose fanatical outbursts had marked the first trial appeared in Pisek as private counsel for the murdered girl's family, the fires of his hatred well stoked for a new performance.

The Pisek trial, it is true, proved more than just a stale reprise of the earlier proceedings at Kuttenberg. The new prosecutor was far more impartial than his predecessor had been, the indictment was not tangled toward ritual-murder charges, and the judges—unlike those at Kuttenberg—attempted neither overtly nor covertly to encourage the blood slander. Moreover, the resources of science were brought into play on Hülsner's behalf. The results of an investigation by the medical faculty of the Czech University in Prague were presented in court; marshaling the the medical evidence in crushing detail, the statement completely demolished the theory that Agnes Hruza's death had been a "ritual murder."

Yet, it was an unequal contest. On one side stood the judges and the men of science, whose only concern was to determine the truth; on the other stood the ranting Deputy, bent on dinning a single idea into the heads of the twelve jurymen. One tirade by the anti-Semitic demagogue went to such extremes of vituperation and ritual-murder demonology that—in an era when public denunciations of the Jews were anything but uncommon—all copies of the speech were confiscated to prevent its publi-

cation. On November 14, the second trial of Leopold
Hülsner ended. Once again, he was sentenced to die by
the rope. And once again his defense counsel, Dr. Zdenko
Aurednizek, entered an immediate plea of nullity.

An extra ingredient had been added to the judicial
mixture in this second trial. At Kuttenberg, Hülsner had
been convicted of murdering only one woman; at Pisek,
he was accused and convicted of murdering two. It was
logical enough: Once you had succeeded in fabricating
a villainous Jewish murderer, why not turn him into a
double murderer? At any rate, it now seemed clear that
Hülsner's doom was finally sealed.

And yet, as it turned out, the anti-Semites were to be
cheated of their prey. From the very beginning, the Polna
affair and the unscrupulous manner in which it was being
exploited had aroused grave misgivings in Austrian judicial
circles. Finally, at Pisek, an extraordinary thing happened:
The very judges who had sentenced Hülsner to death
lodged a petition for clemency. The meaning was clear;
the jury's verdict had left the judges no choice but to
impose the death penalty, but, since they regarded it
as an unjust verdict, their conscience compelled them
to urge that the sentence not be carried out.

After studying the trial record, the Austrian Supreme
Court also recommended mercy for Hülsner. At last,
in June 1901, the process was completed when the Emperor
Franz Joseph, instead of approving the death sentence,
exercised his Imperial right of clemency. Thus, amid outraged cries from the anti-Semites in press and Parliament, Hülsner escaped the gallows. He was not a free
man, for it was not within the Emperor's power to grant
a full pardon. Instead, his sentence was commuted to life
imprisonment at hard labor and he was transferred to
the Pankrac penitentiary.

Some years afterward, the final chapter was written in the story of Leopold Hülsner. After sufficient time had passed for the anti-Semites' wrath to abate and the memory of the case to grow dim, the prison gates were quietly opened and Hülsner was given his freedom. The judicial authorities could not have stated more plainly their opinion of the jury verdicts at Kuttenberg and Pisek.

The real murderer of Agnes Hruza was never found; the anti-Semitic street mobs had effectively covered his tracks. As to Hülsner's subsequent fate little is known. He was said to have made his way to Vienna, where he was given shelter in a home for the poor.

39

EARLY ONE SUNDAY MORNING in June 1899, I took the streetcar to Herzl's home at No. 50 *Karl-Ludwigstrasse* in the Währing section of Vienna. We had matters to discuss pertaining to *Die Welt*. When I arrived, he was strolling along the gravel path in his garden with an editorial colleague from the *Neue Freie Presse*. After the latter had left, we went to his study and settled our business. Then, together with various other written matter, he handed me the manuscript of a long novel and said: "Look through it and see if we can use it." As I was leaving, I met the architect Marmorek, who had just come and was carrying a camera.

That afternoon, Herzl appeared suddenly at my lodgings. I knew at once that he had not come this time, as he had two years before, to invite me out for a leisurely walk. His face showed anxiety and suppressed agitation.

After we had exchanged greetings, he blurted out two words: "The letter!"

"What letter?" I asked.

"Eulenburg's letter . . ." Then, scarcely waiting for me to respond, he went on: 'Have you got the manuscript of that novel I gave you this morning? Perhaps it slipped between the pages."

We went through the manuscript almost page by page, and as we approached the end the look of disappointment grew in Herzl's eyes. I finally turned the last page; there was no sign of a letter. I had never seen Herzl so depressed. He started talking half aloud: "Perhaps I . . . Perhaps it's at the *Türkenstrasse* . . . But I can't imagine how . . ." Then he turned to me: "Let's take a look at the *Welt* office."

We set out for our editorial office on the *Türkenstrasse;* Herzl walked at a faster gait than usual, and I kept pace. When we arrived, I opened up with my key and we scoured every corner; the results were nil. More dejected than ever, Herzl took leave of me in front of the building and started for his parents' home a short distance away.

That was the end of my involvement in the Case of the Vanished Letter. Herzl tells the whole story in his diary under June 5, 1899:

"A curious incident occurred yesterday. I wanted to have Eulenburg's Amsterdam letter photographed . . . lest the only existing copy should be destroyed. The letter had been kept in a safe since October. The day before yesterday, I had it brought to my home for Marmorek. I received it in the garden, then had dinner, and then went into town; since I had a lead article to write (on Dreyfus's homecoming) for the *Neue Freie Presse,* I did not get home until late at night.

"Yesterday morning, Marmorek came out with the camera. I looked for the letter—it wasn't there. I got frightened, rummaged through all the drawers of my desk, etc.—nothing. I had had the manuscript of a novel lying on my desk for months and had just given it to Rosenberger yesterday. Perhaps the letter had strayed into the manuscript. Kremenezky went to Rosenberger's place, to my father's—nothing.

"In the afternoon, I went into town myself, to Rosenberger's, to the *Welt* office, to my parent's house. Nothing! The letter that I had guarded so carefully, that I had wanted to protect for all time against any accident, had gotten lost precisely because of those measures! A tragi-comedy. In whose hands was it at that moment? What a calamity!

"Then my good father advised me to take a look in the garden, too. I went home and hurried to the fir-tree knoll, where I had received the letter the day before yesterday. There on the bench lay the precious letter. By pure chance, the gardener had not been there in the past 24 hours to clean up, nor had our children, who tear up all letters. There had also been no rain, which would have washed out the letter and completely ruined it."

Just what was "Eulenberg's Amsterdam letter," whose disappearance had plunged Herzl into such despair? Count (later Prince) Philipp Eulenburg was at that time the German Ambassador in Vienna and a close confidant of Kaiser Wilhelm II. As we have seen in an earlier chapter, Eulenburg had taken it upon himself to plead the Zionist cause with the Kaiser. On October 1, 1898, during a brief stay in Amsterdam, Herzl received a letter from Eulenburg of such sensational import that it left him stunned. The Count was writing from Rominten,

Germany, where he was a hunting guest of the Kaiser. He had taken advantage of the opportunity to bring up the subject of Zionism, and he was now writing at the Kaiser's behest to inform Herzl that the Kaiser intended shortly to visit Palestine, would like to meet Herzl in Jerusalem, and, indeed, would be disappointed if the meeting failed to materialize.

The high hopes which Herzl placed in the Kaiser were, of course, never realized. Nevertheless, he continued to prize Eulenburg's letter highly. It was documentary proof of why he had made his journey to Palestine and of the Kaiser's pro-Zionist feelings at the time. In the future, should anyone ever ask Herzl why he had gone to Palestine, he could reply: "The Kaiser wanted me to. Here—read the Amsterdam letter."

*   *   *

One day, as I was pursuing my favorite pastime of glancing at bookshop window displays, I spied a paperbound, unmistakably second-hand volume whose cover bore a familiar name: Theodor Herzl. The title was *Neues von der Venus—The Latest About Venus: Causeries and Stories.* Depicted on the cover, between two ornamental plants, was a short column topped by a bust of Venus. Leaning against the column was an elegant, bemoustached gentleman in a dress-suit—a lady-killer, vintage 1887. Several ladies and another gentleman were seated in front of him, listening intently to what he was saying. One of the ladies, whose low-cut back was turned to the reader, was holding the inevitable fan in her left hand and wearing long gloves which reached up over her elbows.

I had never before heard of this particular product of Herzl's pen. I went into the store, purchased *The Latest*

About Venus for a trifling sum, and bore my treasure
home. I immediately read the eighteen *causeries* and
stories, totaling 259 pages, and found them most enter-
taining.

The following day, when I went to Herzl's home on
editorial business, I took *The Latest About Venus* along.
After we had finished our work, I said to him: "I found
a good book yesterday in a second-hand bookstore."

"A good book?"

"By an author whom you surely know."

"Is that so?"

I took *The Latest About Venus* out of my brief-case
and laid it before him in all the glory of its illustrated
cover. Herzl laughed and asked: 'How much did you
pay for it? Ten kreutzers?" I refused to let him belittle
his book, however, and began to praise it. He then
became serious and, after a moment of pensive silence,
said in a regretful tone: "And I write that so easily . . ."
He plainly meant: ". . . so much more easily than many
other things which my journalistic calling compels me
to write."

*   *   *

In my account of the Hülsner case, I omitted any
mention of a lighter footnote which I myself contributed
to that somber drama. It all came about when I decided
to see whether the weapon of ridicule might not help
to puncture the "ritual murder" lie and the knaves and
fools who were propagating it. In my "Week" column
in issue no. 37 of *Die Welt* for 1899, I made a most earnest and solemn announcement: I had, I informed the
reader, stumbled upon an old Hebrew volume of cabal-
istic lore which provided precise instructions for carrying out a ritual murder in the approved style. I then pro-

ceeded to reveal the "seven commandments" of ritual murder—all of them so full of preposterous nonsense that no one could possibly have used them as a recipe for murder.

Any intelligent reader would, of course, recognize at once that my article was intended as satire. However, I hoped that some anti-Semitic fanatic—perhaps the Christian Social Deputy Herr S., who was noted for rushing to the scene whenever a dead body was found in the hope of sniffing out "evidence" of ritual murder—might take it seriously and make a fool of himself. As it happened, some people were taken in—but, instead of anti-Semites, they were Jewish readers of *Die Welt!*

In defense of the gullible ones it should be said that most of them were Eastern European Jews who were not thoroughly familiar with the German language and therefore missed the ironic overtones of my article. Indignant protests started arriving from Russian Poland and other Eastern areas (and, in some cases, even from Vienna and parts of Hungary). I was angrily challenged to name the mysterious book which contained the "seven commandments." I was denounced as a slanderer and a promoter of the ritual-murder lie. There are certain things, I discovered, about which one dare not jest. And I recalled what Herzl had said to me two years earlier: "Never overestimate the reader's education and power of comprehension."

It is hard to say how far the affaiir would have gone had not the widely read Hebrew newspaper *Hamelitz* finally intervened. *Hamelitz* had been receiving letters urging it to give the lie to *Die Welt's* outrageous fabrication. At length, in their issue of October 20, 1899, the editors published a verbatim Hebrew translation of my article, together with an introductory note. After that, the storm began to subside.

Since the arrival of the first protest letters, I had felt that Herzl should be told what was happening. But how was I to tell him? In addition to the Polna affair, he had many other things to occupy his attention: the Dreyfus case, which was back in the news; an unpleasant litigation into which he had been drawn with the former Executive Editor of *Die Welt,* Dr. Lannau; and, of course, his ceaseless work on behalf of the Zionist movement. Finally, during one of Herzl's daily visits to our editorial office, I found an opportune moment and announced: "I have a confession to make."

Herzl looked at me attentively and said: "Out with it! Ease your conscience."

After some hesitation, I told him of the unforeseen repercussions which my little essay had had. Since the article was no longer fresh in his mind, he picked up a copy, settled himself comfortably at his desk, and started to read it. I watched his face for a sign of approval or disapproval, but not a muscle moved as his glance traveled down the page. When he finally reached the end, he laid the magazine down and remarked drily: "Such are the perils of irony." That was all. After a short pause, he asked whether I had sent letters of explanation to those who had protested. I said that I had, and the subject was never mentioned again. All too many "bosses" would have seized the opportunity to deliver a pompous lecture. But that was not Herzl's way.

* * *

As I have mentioned in earlier chapters, Herzl was not stinting in his praise when a contribution to *Die Welt* pleased him, and he often complimented me on what I wrote. Very much of a novice when I first came to the magazine, I gradually traveled the full gamut from brief items to lead articles. Herzl followed this evolution with the satisfaction of a teacher watching his pupil progress. "I foretold it," he said once when something of mine particularly pleased him, referring to an earlier prophecy that I would one day amount to something in a literary way.

It was always a mystery to me how Herzl was able to accomplish, in the time at his disposal, all the things that he took upon himself. Wherever possible, I tried to avoid adding to his burden with *Welt* matters and attended to as much as I could on my own responsibility. Nevetheless, I often sent him manuscripts for his opinion; I knew that his interest in the magazine was as great as ever, and I felt that his editorial influence on it should be maintained. Our office boy took the manuscripts to and from Herzl's home, and he always read them with the utmost care.

Sometimes, after reading a manuscript, Herzl would reach for his pen and dash off a brief note to the author. These messages, when they were addressed to me, seemed all the more precious because they were so obviously the product of sudden impulse.

One such letter, which is still in my possession, is dated July 27, 1899:

"Dear friend,
"Your 'Week' column is magnificent this time.
Best regards,
Th. H."

Another note, dated September 7, 1899, clearly shows the haste with which it sprang from the writer's pen:

"Dear friend,

" 'The Week' is a brilliant success this time!

"I much prefer that you write nothing about—[name omitted]. Use some bit of trivia to fill the empty spot.

"Please have Rudolph take Mintz's authorization to him at once.

Best regards,

TH. HERZL"

Rudolf was our office boy, who had brought the proofs back to me at the print-shop together with Herzl's letter.

At the time of the Hülsner ritual-murder case, with its accompanying anti-Semitic outbreaks, I wrote a lead article for the October 20, 1899 issue of *Die Welt* in which I drew some bitter lessons from what was happening. After reading the proofs, Herzl sent me the following enthusiastic note, dated October 18:

"My dear Rosbgr,

"I am proud of you, for I feel that you have learned something from me.

Yours,

TH. H."

I was proud that he took pride in me—particularly because the hastily penciled lines plainly testified that what he had set down on paper was his first, spontaneous reaction.

40

DIE WELT NEVER PROSPERED in a financial way. Its subscription list was not large enough even to cover the magazine's costs, much less put it on a paying basis.

The reasons for this state of affairs were obvious. *Die Welt*'s potential readership was limited from the very start. To begin with, it was a Jewish magazine which aimed at Jewish readers. In addition, it was a special kind of Jewish magazine which espoused a special creed, that of Zionism; this had the effect of further restricting its appeal.

There was also what might be called a socio-economic factor in *Die Welt*'s failure to thrive. The yearly subscription price was six florins for Austrian readers and eight for foreign readers. Six Austrian florins were then equivalent to half an English pound—surely a moderate amount. Yet, for the mass of struggling European Jews a magazine subscription was a luxury which could ill be afforded. And, ironically, it was precisely the wealthier Jews who had no reason to support *Die Welt*. A well-to-do Jew leading a comfortable existence in Austria or Germany was the last person to subscribe to a magazine which preached Jewish emigration to Palestine for the purpose of founding a new state.

To all these factors, finally, was added the widespread feeling that *Die Welt* was chasing a phantom. It was regarded by many as Jules Verne in magazine form—the mouthpiece for a movement that was trying to organize a trip to the moon.

Nevertheless, *Die Welt* always had far more readers than paying subscribers. The reason was the coffee houses and

Zionist societies. In Vienna, Berlin, Lemberg, Czernowitz, Breslau, Brünn and other cities, at least one café proprietor subscribed to *Die Welt*. From one Friday to the next, when the new issue came out, the single copy passed from hand to hand among the patrons—many of whom in most coffee houses were Jewish. The Zionist societies played a similar role. By the time the Second Zionist Congress convened in Basle in the summer of 1898, there were 913 such groups throughout the world. A year later, the number had risen to approximately 1,300. In each of the Zionist societies, a single copy of *Die Welt* circulated among dozens of readers. Thus, the number of the magazine's subscribers was in no sense an index of its success in spreading the Zionist idea.

Despite its deficit, which Herzl largely made up out of his private funds, *Die Welt* paid well for articles in the early days. Herzl was anxious to present literary names of the first rank in the magazine's columns, and in order to do so he had to match the rates of other, more affluent publications. Ironically, however, many of these prominent contributors were no sooner induced to write for *Die Welt* than they took refuge in pseudonyms. The times were unfortunately such that a writer might fear being compromised if he should openly identify himself with the Zionist movement.

Max Nordau was one who never wrote for *Die Welt* under any name but his own, regardless of the consequences. On the other hand, Wilhelm Goldbaum of the *Neue Freie Presse* used a variety of pseudonyms. Despite the distinguished name he had made for himself as a writer on literary and political subjects, he could not take the risk of appearing openly in *Die Welt*. If the *Presse*'s anti-Semitic competitors had found out that not only Herzl (who was, of course, an editor of the *Presse*) but also Goldbaum was associated with *Die Welt,* their shouts of glee would have filled the heavens and Goldbaum's employers would have given him the choice of severing his connection with the Zionist paper or losing his job.

On various occasions, as we have seen, Herzl's own activities with *Die Welt* brought him into conflict with the publishers of the *Neue Freie Presse.* He had hoped, when he founded his magazine, that it would be enough of a financial success to make him independent of the *Presse.* In that respect, *Die Welt* proved a disappointment to him.

41

NOW I COME TO A CHAPTER in these reminiscences which affords me no pleasure in the telling: that which deals with my resignation from *Die Welt.*

Herzl's expenditures on various Zionist activities were gradually draining his financial reserves. At the same time, his complete absorption in Zionist work left him little time for more lucrative pursuits in the field of *belles lettres. Die Welt* was, of course, one of his heaviest financial burdens. At last, he reached the point where the burden could no longer be carried; He was forced to turn over the financing of *Die Welt* to a number of wealthy individuals in the Zionist movement.

I have no idea to what extent the consortium that undertook to put *Die Welt* on its feet drew upon private funds and to what extent upon the resources of the Zionist movement as such. I know only that one fine day a little man with a large black beard marched into our office and

started walking up and down, all the while delivering himself of a series of captious comments which seemed directed
partly to himself alone and partly to the outside world.
His entire bearing very plainly said one thing: I pay the
bills—consequently, I have the right to be here and to
say what I please.

This visit proved only the curtain-raiser. On May 31,
1900, one of the members of the Vienna Zionist "Action
Committee" appeared at the *Welt* office and, with visible
embarrassment, expressed the desire to speak to me privately. My guest was the publisher of a small technical
journal which made a profit from the open commercial
notices it carried in its advertising section as well as from
the concealed ones in the rest of the magazine; on the
strength of this link with the world of journalism, the
new masters of *Die Welt* had given him the assignment
of negotiating with me in editorial matters. Among the
sundry pieces of intelligence brought by this emissary was
one which left me aghast and indignant: Herzl was no
longer to be my ultimate authority in editing *Die Welt!*
Henceforth, I was to receive my instructions from another.

I said nothing when the news was broken to me. It
seemed pointless to remonstrate with the man who stood
before me, painfully groping for words as he discharged
his disagreeable mission. But the moment he had left I
sat down and, in the full flush of my wrath, wrote Herzl
a long letter in which I offered my candid opinion of
various members of the "Action Committee" and com-
plained bitterly of the treatment I had received. I em-
phasized in particular that, in editorial matters, I was
unwilling to take orders from anyone but Herzl himself.
Here are some portions of my impassioned message:

". . . I am permitted to go on writing articles under
----'s supervision. Call me conceited and swell-headed, if

you like. But I will not defer to the censorship and the vote of Herr ---- . . . Nor to that of ---, whose manuscripts, when he favored us with them, I always had to revise drastically so that they would read like good German. You know, Herr Doktor, that I have never objected when you ripped half pages out of my 'Week' column; I have calmly accepted every correction, every criticism. But I would make myself ridiculous if I credulously swallowed the advice of the new editorial committee. And later on I would feel embarrassed to think that I had allowed masters such as these to rap me on the knuckles . . .

"I am very sorry, dear Herr Doktor, that I have to write you this letter. You are, after all, in no way to blame for the decisions of Messrs. ---, ---, etc. And if *Die Welt* had remained your property, none of this would have happened . . . I realize that, under the pressure of constant disagreement, you finally had to let the gentlemen have their way, since, after all, their shares gave them the right to decide things."

Herzl replied at once:

"Vienna, June 1, 1900

"My dear Rosenberger,

"Your letter causes me pain, for you know how highly I have thought of you over the years. I have no more to say in the matter.

"Just this hasty note today, since I have work to do for the *N.F.P.* We'll talk about it later.

As ever, cordially yours,

TH. HERZL"

Herzl's letter confirmed what I already knew: He had "no more say" at *Die Welt*. I spent the next day, a Satur-

day, reflecting on the situation. On Sunday, I wrote to
Herzl again:

"*Vienna, June 3, 1900*

"*Dear Herr Doktor:*

"This morning, I informed - - - that I was resigning from
the editorial staff on July 1. . . . After you left the staff,
Herr Doktor, nothing remained anyway to bind me to
Die Welt. If anything—apart from the Zionist idea—has
made *Die Welt* dear to me, it has been you alone. For the
most part, I have written only for you; you have been
looking over my shoulder as I wrote . . ."

As Herzl had promised in his letter, we had a number
of talks about what had happened. One of the first things
he said to me was: "The fact that our official relations
have been broken off does not affect our friendship." He
also commented on the attitude of the new committee
which supervised *Die Welt:* "I don't think they meant
to offend you." "Neither do I now," I replied, "I may have
been mistaken. But I can't accept the idea that someone
else is now to be my boss and give me orders."

Herzl gave an unexpected proof of his friendship by
inviting me to write light articles for the *Neue Freie
Presse.* He undoubtedly had several motives in doing so:
He knew, of course, that the money would be by no means
unwelcome to me. He probably felt, too, that by winning
me *entrée* to so distinguished a journal he would be opening the gates to a literary career for me. In spite of his
earlier remark, however, I suspect that his offer was also
intended partly as a demonstrative gesture against the new
Welt committee.

Herzl was also anxious for me to retain some connection
with *Die Welt,* and, after I had ceased to be Editor, he
asked me to write a special article. A flood of Rumanian

Jews, despairing of ever finding a decent existence in their homeland, was then passing through Vienna, bound for the New World. At Herzl's suggestion, I spoke to some of these unfortunates—mostly artisans and their families—at a restaurant and a Talmud-Torah school where they were being sheltered. The result of this moving experience was an article entitled "Nomads" in issue no. 28 of *Die Welt* for 1900. For the time being, that was my last contribution to the magazine.

My work for the *Neue Freie Presse* amounted to very little. One of the two editors and publishers, Dr. Eduard Bacher, was kindly disposed toward me; but the other, Moriz Benedikt, was not eager to admit yet another *Welt* alumnus to the columns of his paper. "I like it, but Benedikt turned it down," Herzl said to me once as he returned one of my manuscripts. On several other occasions, he himself felt that articles I had submitted were unsuitable for the *Presse*. I was extremely grateful to Herzl for the efforts he made for me, but it quickly became apparent that success lay in some other direction.

The question was whether I should continue writing or return reluctantly to the University. In a brief, laudatory announcement in *Die Welt*, my good friend Moritz Zobel had informed the readers that I was resigning in order to complete my medical studies; and, in fact, I had told him that I might do so. On the other hand, I had made promising connections with several other Viennese papers and was extremely loath to give up journalism altogether. I finally decided on a compromise: I would resume my studies and, at the same time, continue to write.

I promptly enrolled in a course in internal medicine which was conducted at the General Hospital on the *Alserstrasse*. Yet, as I listened to the lectures and watched the practical demonstrations, I realized that I was following the proceedings as much from a writer's as from a medical student's viewpoint. Before long, I had produced a fairly long *feuilleton* which I entitled "The Island of Aesculapius." (The reference was to the hospital, standing in the midst of the great city.) I took it to Herzl, who shortly thereafter informed me that he liked it and that it had been accepted for the *feuilleton* section of the *Neue Freie Presse*. He also said he was glad that I was back at my medical studies.

Yet, my *feuilleton* was fated never to appear; instead, it lay in some corner, forgotten by everyone but its author. My latest essay into medicine proved equally abortive. After the course at the General Hospital ended, I gave up any further preparations for the examinations and began hearkening more and more to the siren song of journalism.

42

HAVING ONCE MORE laid aside the scalpel for the pen, I soon established myself as a regular contributor to the *Illustriertes Wiener Extrablatt,* a widely read Viennese daily. When I told Herzl of my success, I expected at least a mild reproof for abandoning my studies. Instead, however, he seemed pleasantly surprised.

One of the *Extrablatt's* two editors-in-chief, Julius Bauer, was a Zionist sympathizer whom I had met two years earlier. I began contributing to virtually every department of his paper, including the *feuilleton* section. I also made occasional forays into the columns of other Viennese newspapers (without, I might add, letting Julius

Bauer into the secret). And at length, drawn by a kind of irresistible gravitational pull, I found myself once again in contact with the *Neue Freie Presse*. Looking back now over the years, I have no doubt of what it was that drew me back to the *Presse*: Far more than the desire to write for the greatest newspaper in Vienna, it was the knowledge that, if I became a frequenter of the *Presse's* editorial offices, I would again be in close personal contact with the man who had become so great an influence in my life during the three years I had worked by his side at *Die Welt*. At all events, in August 1901 (still unbeknownst to anyone at the *Extrablatt!*) I started contributing unsigned brief items to the *Presse's* local-news section.

For a time, my relations with the *Presse* were so close that Dr. Bacher held out some hope of a position for me on the editorial staff. I was eager to discuss the matter with Herzl at the next opportunity—not that I doubted his support and good will; rather, I wanted to make it plain that I was not going "over his head" by dealing with Dr. Bacher. The opportunity soon presented itself; on October 8, as I was coming out of Dr. Bacher's office, I unexpectedly encountered Herzl. He was visibly pleased to see me and promptly took me into his office for a chat. However, the conversation didn't go at all as I had planned. I had looked forward to a calm, matter-of-fact discussion of my prospects. Instead, under the emotional impact of the sudden meeting, I found myself utterly disconcerted and self-conscious. Just as in the early days of my acquaintance with Herzl, I felt a schoolboy in the presence of a revered teacher—scarcely able to speak and then only with a trembling voice. As a result, little of what I had meant to say ever passed my lips.

In the end, the hoped-for position on the *Presse* failed to materialize, and I started once more devoting most of my energy to the *Extrablatt*. My work for that journal could scarcely have been further removed from the intellectual realm in which I had moved during my *Welt* days. On one occasion, I interviewed a lady wrestler to obtain material for a *feuilleton*. Another time, having heard that the Imperial executioner had recently employed a new technique in dispatching a murderer, I visited the gentleman at his Vienna home, questioned him on the fine points of his profession, and even let him demonstrate his methods on my own neck (up to a point, of course). Unfortunately, Julius Bauer found the resulting article a trifle too gruesome for the *Extrablatt's* readers, but I succeeded in selling it to the Prague *Tagblatt*. During the Fasching carnival time, I covered gala balls from one end of Vienna to the other for the *Extrablatt,* and once I regaled our readers with the extraordinary talents of the performers in a local flea circus.

This sort of activity had a certain charm, of course, but I became increasingly aware that I was caught in a vicious circle of triviality. I was still wrestling irresolutely with my doubts when, one day in October 1902, I chanced to meet Herzl near the *St. Peters-Platz*. I gladly accepted his invitation to walk a while with him.

"How are you?" he asked. "What are you doing at the *Extrablatt?*"

As I described the work I was doing, I was overcome by the realization of how trivial it all sounded and I tried to lend it a humorous note. But Herzl clearly saw nothing funny in it. He had stopped and was listening in utter dismay. "Let's go back ... in there," he said finally. "I have something to say to you."

We turned into the St. *Peters-Platz,* which was virtually deserted. Then Herzl cut loose at me.

"What you are doing," he began, "is nothing but loafing. . . ."

As he spoke, we walked slowly back and forth; from time to time, he stopped and looked me full in the face.

"You are working at one of the most despised of all trades," Herzl continued. "When they need you, perhaps to write a publicity puff, they come to you and are very polite, but then they turn around and mutter between their teeth: 'Hack journalist!' And how pitifully dependent you are on the publisher of the paper! You are eternally at his mercy.

"Think, too, of your old age. One of the saddest sights is the old newspaperman who, exhausted by years of work and in need of rest, must go toiling on and on in the treadmill until finally the publisher throws him on the scrapheap. You are young and have no family; you can still get out of it. If you want me to speak to you in the future and to respect you, then leave the paper and get your medical degree. Once you have that, you can write as many novels and stories as you like in your spare time, and your work will be infinitely better when you no longer have to adapt it to the needs of a newspaper and to the taste and understanding of its readers."

Before taking leave of me, Herzl held my hand a few seconds longer than usual and looked at me as though at a prodigal son who was being brought back to the right path. His words had deeply affected me, though all I said in reply was: "Thank you, Herr Doktor. You are very right." As he went, he repeated once more: "Rosenberger, if you want me to greet you on the street, get your medical degree."

43

A MONG MY VIENNESE RELATIVES
were some very wealthy people, the
owners of a large glass-manufacturing concern, S. Reich
& Co. Shortly after my meeting with Herzl, I wrote to my
cousin Julius Reich, who was an extremely kind-hearted,
generous man. His reply was as I had expected: He would
be happy to give me the financial aid I need in order to
finish my medical studies. I promptly went to see Julius
Bauer at the *Extrablatt* and obtained a leave of absence
for the duration of my studies. I decided not to tell Herzl
of my plans until I could offer proof that this time I was
really in earnest.

At the beginning, it was a little difficult to adjust once
again to the lecture halls and dissection rooms. By mid-
December, however, just two months after I returned to
the University, I had passed the first examinations in the
second *Rigorosum*. By the following May, I was so confident of ultimate success that I wrote Herzl to tell him
how rapidly his advice had borne fruit. Little realizing
how many other cares were preoccupying him at that
moment, I enthusiastically enclosed a number of examination certificates in my letter as evidence of my accomplishments. I received the following reply:

"Vienna, May 20, 1903
"My dear friend Rosenberger,

"It makes me feel very proud to know that you thought
so highly of my advice. I think you will first realize at
some future time what good advice it was.

"If I may be permitted a further word of advice now,
I would suggest that, as soon as your examinations are

over, you spend the rest of your volunteer year in the Navy
and then serve for a while with the Lloyd line as a ship's
doctor. You will see the world, and the result will be fine
books which I am already looking forward to—provided
that I live to see them.

"There is only one thing which I cannot forgive you:
that, frightfully overburdened as I am, you should force
me to reply to you and even send me certificates. . . .

"*With cordial regards, as always very sincerely,*

HERZL

The last sentence in the letter, which contrasted so
glaringly with the earlier friendly remarks, left me at first
utterly crushed. It seemed incomprehensible that Herzl
should begrudge the five minutes required to dictate a
brief note after he had spent a half hour the previous
October urging me to mend my ways. Gradually, however,
I came to realize that his reproach was really a cry of pain
from a man laboring under an almost unbearable burden.
Only later did I learn of all the varied Zionist enterprises
in which he had been embroiled at just that time: of the
letters he was writing to Russian, Portuguese, British,
Austrian and Turkish statesmen, as well as the letter he
was having Baroness Suttner write to the Tsar.

Some time afterward, I met Herzl on the street. "Ah,"
he exclaimed in the best of good humor, "here is our
doctor!" "Not yet," I replied with reference to the prematurely bestowed title, "but soon, I hope." It was apparent
from his genuinely cordial manner that he had already
forgotten the letter and the momentary annoyance it had
expressed.

Herzl quickly brought the conversation around to my
prospective career as a ship's doctor. This was actually an
old ambition of mine which had spurred me on from the

very start of my medical studies; my imagination had been
particularly stirred by the tales I heard from several young
doctor friends who had spent some time on Austrian
Lloyd steamers. Now Herzl was speaking of the life of a
ship's doctor with an enthusiasm that seemed almost to
suggest that he would have chosen that career for himself
if fate had not cast him in a different role. "Become a
Pierre Loti!" he said to me, referring to the famous French
writer of sea stories.

"Thank you for your good opinion," I began depre-
catingly, "but. . . ."

He interrupted me: "Do you get seasick?"

'I don't know. I've never been on a seagoing ship. In
fact, I've never seen the sea."

"Ah," he said regretfully. "You've never seen the
sea. . . ." Then he remarked: "Avoiding seasickness is a
matter of will-power . . . to a large extent."

At that point, I noticed that Herzl's attention had
shifted to a man who was walking rapidly in our direction.
Both of them lifted their hats at the same moment. The
stranger, a distinguished-looking man, did not stop, but
he whispered a few words to Herzl as he passed. All at
once, Herzl became silent and pensive. Seasickness and
ship's doctors were suddenly far from his mind. When I
finally interrupted his thoughts to say goodbye, he started
up as though from a dream and said: 'Drop in at *Die Welt*
some time—we'll talk about things."

Long afterward, the publication of Herzl's diaries solved
the riddle of the distinguished-looking stranger for me.
He had been the Portuguese Ambassador to Vienna, Count
Paraty. Some two weeks before, Herzl had asked the Count
to inquire whether his Government would be willing to
make a suitable tract of land available for the settlement

of at least 50,000 Jewish families. He had in mind Mozambique, the Portuguese colony on the southeastern coast of Africa. However, Mozambique was not his ultimate objective, as his diaries revealed:

"I want to try to acquire this unproductive land from the financially straitened Portuguese Government for a chartered company by promising to cover the deficit and later pay tribute. However, I want Mozambique only for trading purposes, so that I can obtain in exchange from the British Government the entire Sinai Peninsula, with Nile water for summer and winter, and perhaps Cyprus as well—and free at that!"

The words which the Portuguese Ambassador had whispered to Herzl in the street were: *"Pas de reponse"*—no reply as yet from his Government.

*   *   *

Herzl's father, Jacob, had died on June 9, 1902 at the the age of 67.

In the early days of *Die Welt*, as we have seen, the elder Herzl had charge of the magazine's business affairs. Some years before that, he rendered his son a valuable service when the latter was first establishing himself on the staff of the *Neue Freie Presse*. At the beginning of 1892, after Theodor Herzl had completed his four-month trial period as Paris correspondent for the *Presse*, Jacob Herzl in Vienna handled negotiations with the paper on the terms of permanent employment. He showed himself shrewd in defending his son's interests—a task made easier by the fact that his dealings were chiefly with Dr. Eduard Bacher, an admirer of Herzl's literary skill who was eager to obtain the latter's services. The result was an agreement providing for an annual salary of 12,000 francs. with an anticipated future increase and an additional 100 francs for each *feuilleton.* This put Herzl in the top pay brackets in Viennese journalism.

The *Presse's* Editor-in-chief, Dr. Bacher, not only had a keen professional appreciation of the merit of Herzl's *feuilletons,* lead articles and correspondence; he was also personally fond of their author. When Herzl launched upon his Zionist venture, Dr. Bacher was dismayed. He felt that, instead of dedicating himself fully to a literary career that might one day bring him great renown, Herzl was dissipating his energies in the pursuit of a will-o'-the-wisp. If he were alive today, the good-hearted Dr. Bacher would undoubtedly have second thoughts on the subject.

44

M Y MEDICAL STUDIES MOVED steadily forward; I successfully completed the second *Rigorosum,* leaving only the third and last to be hurdled. Then, all at once, I suffered a recurrence of an old fever: the urge to write. Since the medical degree now seemed firmly in my grasp, I decided to yield to temptation and soon found myself playing three roles at once: those of medical student, contributor to the *Extrablatt* . . . and, once again, contributor to *Die Welt.*

My first *Welt* article during this new phase was a *feuilleton* which appeared in the July 3, 1903 issue under the title, "Table Talk at the Weidhof Café." In "Table Talk," which was the first of a series of columns published under the same title, three Jewish coffee-house patrons discussed the plight of the Jews in the light of recent anti-Semitic outbreaks in Eastern Europe. Soon afterward, I received the following letter from Herzl:

"Alt-Aussee, July 13, 1903

"Dear friend Rosenberger:

" 'Table Talk at the Weidhof Café' is good, but you must be very careful with a column like that. That sort of thing can be a success if, particularly at the beginning, it is always scintillating; but it can also arouse furious indignation if it misfires a few times. I therefore advise you to remain as topical as possible, not to pluck at the same string all the time, and above all not to feel that the conclusion must always be a Zionist one, *i.e.*, that you must wind up each time with something from the Basle Program.

"Assimilation provides such broad scope for humorous treatment that you can't lack for material. Among other things, the correspondence from Schlochau-Flatow in the last issue of *Die Welt*, in which the Jewish rabbi Levin recommends voting for the anti-Semite, was very amusing. That's the kind of material that can be handled in a joshing manner. I don't think you should discuss Kishinev any more; it's starting to become a declamatory piece . . .

"With cordial regards,
Your faithful reader,
HERZL"

I was deeply moved by the fact that, amid all his other concerns, Herzl had taken the time to read my *feuilleton* and offer his comments on it.

Kishinev, to which Herzl had referred in his letter, was a city in the Russian province of Bessarabia which several weeks previously had been the scene of a bloody pogrom. I had written my first "Table Talk" article at a time when we were all still trembling in helpless rage at the Kishinev massacre and the official encouragement for not wishing any further mention of the subject in *Die Welt*. He intended to go to Russia in order to plead for better treatment of the harassed Russian Jews and, at the same time, to state the case for Zionism. Three weeks later, he did in fact journey to St. Petersburg; he had conversations with leading Russian statesmen and obtained reassuring promises, some of them even in writing. Yet, within a few years Tsarist Russia was the scene of new pogroms which outdid Kishinev in savagery. . . .

* * *

At last, the great day arrived on which I took and passed my final medical examination. I still remember the feeling of overwhelming relief with which I left this last barrier behind me. I promptly notified my parents, who had probably despaired of ever seeing me obtain my degree, and had cards printed for distribution when the ceremony took place: "Erwin Rosenberg has the honor to inform you that he was awarded the degree of Doctor of Medicine on Wednesday, September 30, 1903, at 12 noon in the banquet hall of the Imperial University."

My card brought the following letter from Herzl:

"Alt-Aussee, September 30, 1903
"My dear Rosenberger:

"Accept my heartiest congratulations on your degree, with which I flatter myself that I had something to do. Only later will you realize how right I was in urging you to get it. Now you have a passport with which you can

travel far away from that ignoble trade. I hope to see
you in Vienna and talk with you about your future, in
which, as you know, I take a friendly interest.

                    "With cordial regards,

                              Yours truly,

                                    HERZL"

"That ignoble trade" was, of course, a reference to the
kind of hack journalism from which Herzl's words of warning had helped me to extricate myself the previous October. The epithet was in no sense directed at the journalistic
profession as such.

45

THE SIXTH ZIONIST CONGRESS
was held in Basle from August 23 to
28, 1903. It opened amid fervid demonstrations of the
delegates' loyalty to their leader, Theodor Herzl. Yet,
before it was over the Congress had given Herzl many
painful hours.

Herzl's opening address contained two sensational reve-
lations which appeared to evoke unanimous enthusiasm
among his listeners. Here are his words as they appear
in the official record of the Congress:

"Events which are well known to all of you made it
necessary for me to travel to Russia in the interests of
the Jewish people. I had a welcome opportunity to meet
members of the Government there, and I can say that I
encountered a certain degree of understanding of our
Zionist endeavors and also heard expression of a desire

to do something decisive for us. I confess, incidentally, that I did not take it amiss. I spoke not only for the Zionists but for all the Russian Jews. [Thunderous applause.] I pleaded for some improvement in their sad condition and was assured that such relief will soon be given consideration.

"Even more important were the assurances I obtained with regard to the Zionist movement. I am in a position to state that the Russian Government has no desire to place obstacles in the path of Zionism provided it remains, as hitherto, peaceful and lawful in character. [Thunderous, prolonged applause.] Furthermore, the Russian Government is willing to help meet the costs of an emigration directed by us Zionists.

"Finally—and this is unquestionably the most important fact of all—the Russian Government is willing to use its influence to support our efforts to obtain Palestine from His Majesty the Sultan. [Thunderous, repeatedly renewed applause. The audience rises. Hats and handkerchiefs are waved. Cheering.]"

This was surely startling news: Scarcely more than a few months after the Kishnev pogrom, the Tsar's government had declared its willingness to aid the Zionist cause. Yet, Herzl had made what was perhaps an even more spectacular disclosure earlier in his speech. He began by announcing the failure of a British-supported attempt to secure a piece of land on the Sinai Peninsula for large-scale Jewish settlement. Then he reported what had happened after the British ministers learned of the collapse of the Sinai project:

"They at once offered to grant a different territory for Jewish colonization instead of the earlier one. The new territory does not have the value from an historical, poetic, religious and Zionist point of view that the Sinai Peninsula would have had; but I am certain that the Congress, as representative of the Jewish masses, will accept the new offer, too, with the deepest gratitude. The proposal means an autonomous Jewish settlement in East Africa with a Jewish administration, a Jewish local government and a Jewish official at its head—all, of course, under British sovereignty and supervision. . . .

"I do not wish to anticipate the Congress's views on the policy that the Zionist movement should pursue with regard to these proposals; however, although the Jewish people, needless to say, can have no ultimate goal other than Palestine [Thunderous, prolonged, repeatedly re-newed applause in the hall and in the galleries], and al-though our views about the land of our fathers are and must remain unalterable, whatever the fate of the proposal may be, the Congress will still recognize how tremendously the negotiations with the British Government have fur-thered our movement. [Lively applause.] . . . To be sure, this is not Zion and never can be. It is merely a stop-gap colonization project—although, be it noted, one which is based on nationhood and statehood. [Thunderous ap-plause.] On the strength of this, we cannot and will not give our masses the signal for departure. It is and remains only an emergency measure. . . ."

Thus, Herzl had made it perfectly clear that the East African plan was purely a temporary expedient and that the ultimate objective was still Palestine. And the end of his speech, according to the official record, was marked by a standing ovation.

On the second day of the Congress, Max Nordau gave his eloquent support to the plan:

"Before the immutable goal of Jewish settlement of Palestine is attained, there can be only a resting place along the way and only provisional work: the building of a temporary structure for our hundreds of thousands of unfortunate brothers—whether Zionists or not is quite unimportant; it is enough that they are Jews [Lively applause]—who, unlike us settled ones, cannot wait, who are already wanderers, who are already being flung to and fro from continent to continent and from ocean to ocean like the shuttle of a loom, who will perish unless we do something to save them. Until we can provide these hundreds of thousands with a permanent dwelling place, we must, so to speak, establish a lodging house for them. [Thunderous applause.]

"I would regard as such a lodging house the colony for which the British Government is willing to grant us land under certain conditions. To be sure, it would be a very special kind of lodging house, just as everything that we Jews undertake as a people has a unique quality. It would be a lodging house that not only provided its occupaants with momentary food and shelter but also served as a medium of political and historical education, an educational medium that accustomed the Jews and the world to a thought which had been foreign to them for thousands of years and to many of them had become unbearably distasteful: that we Jews are a nation, a nation that is ready, willing and able to assume all the common responsibilities of a civilized, independent nation. [Thunderous, prolonged applause.]"

As Nordau concluded his speech amid enthusiasm comparable to that which had greeted Herzl the previous day, it must have seemed to every visitor sitting in the gallery that only a word from Herzl was needed now in order to launch a general migration to East Africa. Actually, Herzl had no intention of acting precipitately; he asked the Congress merely to appoint a committee to study the matter and to send a group of experts to East Africa to see whether the area was suitable for settlement. And yet, contrary to all expectations, this modest request encountered violent opposition. Many of the delegates flatly rejected not only the East African plan itself but even the idea of examining it.

There were a number of reasons for this attitude. Despite the repeated explanations by Herzl and Nordau that the proposed venture was to be purely temporary, some delegates mistakenly supposed that they were being forced to choose between East Africa and Palestine. Another group, the Zionist conservatives, adamantly refused to discuss Jewish colonization anywhere but in Palestine under any circumstances. Finally, there were those who feared that the "temporary" East African project, once it was under way, would gradually push all thoughts of Palestine into the background. A factor which contributed to the general misunderstanding was the multiplicity of languages used at the Congress; the debate was conducted in Germaan, Russian, Yiddish, Hebrew, English and French, and even the interpreters could not bring perfect order out of the resulting chaos.

Ironically, it was Max Nordau who unwittingly supplied the opponents of the East Africa plan with valuable ammunition. When Nordau described the proposed haven for Europe's Jews as a "lodging house," a *Nachtasyl,* he could not have chosen a worse simile. For *Nachtasyl* was precisely the title under which Maxim Gorky's grim play, *The Lower Depths,* was then appearing in a German version; and many of the delegates at Basle had seen the ghastly inn which Gorky depicted, with its company of drunkards, convicts, murderers and trollops. The oppositionists were well aware, of course, that Nordau had not had a Gorkian "lodging house" in mind for the Jews. However, they found it polemically convenient to draw a false analogy, and they exploited the point to the full.

When the time for a vote finally arrived, the atmosphere was charged with tension. It seemed to many that the very existence of the Zionist movement was at stake, and Herzl made a personal appeal to the delegates to be mindful of their great responsibility:

"We owe a debt of thanks for the splendid offer which we have received; we cannot express it merely with words or by waving hats and handkerchiefs. In a serious matter, we must show our gratitude first of all by treating it seriously, and it is essential to the seriousness of this treatment that an expedition be sent out to investigate, without prejudice . . . to the principles of our movement and without anticipating the Congress's decision on the colonization itself. I wish to call your attention particularly to the concluding portion of this proposal before I have it read: The decision on the colonization of East Africa is reserved to a congress which will be specially convened for that purpose."

The results of the vote showed 295 in favor of the proposal, 178 opposed, and a substantial number of abstentions. After announcing the outcome, Herzl stressed once again to the delegates that the decision they had just made committed them only to study the British offer, not to accept it. Nevertheless, the vote taken on August 26, 1903 caused bitter internal strife within the Zionist movement and greatly saddened the remaining days of Herzl's life. For the first time, he heard his aims challenged and misrepresented by adherents of the cause for which he had worked so selflessly. It was only through his infinite patience and wisdom that the rift was finally healed and discipline restored.

* * *

In the weeks that followed the Sixth Congress, I wrote a number of reports on the East African scheme for the *Illustriertes Wiener Extrablatt.* (Incidentally, it was much to the credit of the *Extrablatt's* two editors-in-chief, Julius Löwy and Julius Bauer, that they published my articles; the other Viennese papers which were edited by Jews generally made a point of avoiding any mention of the Zionist movement.) I supported Herzl's position that it was neither intelligent nor courteous to reject the British offer without first examining it. This was particularly so because the offer had been made by Joseph Chamberlain, the British Colonial Secretary, who was a good friend of Herlz's and of the Jewish people. It had been during a tour of East Africa, as Chamberlain himself later recounted it, that the thought occurred to him: "Here is a country which will suit Dr. Herzl."

I sent clippings of my articles to Herzl and received the one-sentence reply: "My sincere thanks for the propaganda you are conducting for us *in partibus infidelium.*" The Latin phrase, a formula signifying "in the lands of the infidels" which was affixed to the titles of certain Roman Catholic bishops, was intended as a humorous reference to the fact that the *Extrablatt's* readers were predominantly non-Jewish. When I next met Herzl, I said: "Herr Doktor, I thank you for naming me a bishop." He was puzzled at first, then laughed when I reminded him of his note.

There were few occasions after that when I saw Herzl laugh. His face had always had an underlying seriousness

in its expression; now, after six years of labor and heart-
ache in the cause of Zionism, it had become the face of
an unhappy man. Where, I wondered sorrowfully, was
the eager, optimistic Herzl I had known in the early *Welt*
days at No. 6 *Berggasse?*

46

MONDAY, JULY 4, 1904
was one of the most
tragic days of my life. On that day, the news reached Vienna that Theodor Herzl was dead.

Die Welt mailed copies of the following brief notice to
its subscribers:

"The Zionist Action Committee announces with deep
grief the death of its President, Dr. Theodor Herzl, who
passed away after a long illness on Sunday, July 3, 1904,
at 5 p.m., in Edlach, Lower Austria.

"The burial will take place on Thursday, July 7, 1904,
at 10 a.m., at the Döbling Cemetery (Jewish section).
Services at the home of the deceased: Vienna-Währing,
No. 29, *Haizingergasse.*"

The overwhelming grief into which the news of Herzl's
death plunged me was made greater by its complete un-
expectedness. None of us had known that his heart was
slowly failing under the inhuman burden which he imposed upon it. Moreover, the immediate cause of death,
pneumonia, had been a matter of but a few days, and the
Zionist Action Committee in Vienna had successfully concealed the fact that its leader was gravely ill in Edlach.

It was impossbile for me at first to grasp the fact that Herzl was no longer alive, that I would never again speak to him. The sense of loss left me dazed and bewildered. When the body was laid out in Herzl's home, I rode out to Währing. Frau Herzl smiled weakly as she greeted me, her eyes red from weeping. The coffin lay in Herzl's study, with six unlit candles in tall silver candle-sticks on either side. The walls and windows of the room were hung with black drapery; crape-covered electric lights and an oil lamp at the head of the coffin provided only feeble illumination. As I stood before the coffin, which was guarded by black-clad members of Vienna's Zionist student societies, I asked myself incredulously: Were all the splendid, unique and infinitely varied things that Theodor Herzl had meant to us now confined within this narrow black box?

On July 7, the day of the funeral, I went to Herzl's home well before the time set for the ceremony. Others had arrived even earlier so that they might spend a last few hours near the man whom they had loved and revered. The throng of mourners grew steadily larger. Men and women of all ages filed past the coffin, pausing a moment to say farewell before passing into the adjoining room to offer their sympathy to Herzl's widow and mother, then leaving the house so that the seemingly endless procession could continue. Many were damp-eyed or audibly sobbing; some hesitated before entering the room where the body lay, as though striken by awe at the majesty of death—and at the majesty of the man who had died. I vividly recall the behavior of Dr. Alexander Mintz, a former member of the Action Committee, whom I had always considered a calm, undemonstrative person. When he reached the entrance to the room and saw the coffin, he stood rooted to the spot as if first comprehending the fact of Herzl's death. Then, suddenly, forgetting everyone about him, he clutched at his face and shook with convulsive sobbing.

As the time for the religious service approached, the members of the Action Committee stationed themselves on both sides of the coffin, over which was draped the blue-and-white Zionist flag. From outside came the sound of a vast multitude of persons—thousands who had come from near and far to escort Herzl's body to its final resting place. At the appointed hour, the rabbi, the cantor and the choir arrived. Until then, I had been able to hold my emotions at least partially in check. When the cantor began to intone the prayer for the dead, however, my self-control deserted me and I wept openly. At the same moment, in the next room, Herzl's mother uttered a heart-rending cry: "Theodor, my son, my son. . . ." And through it all could be heard the sobbing of his widow.

I remember relatively little of the journey to the cemetery, during which I walked, almost somnambulistically, a short distance behind the plain black hearse. When we arrived, I helped to bear the coffin to the grave. Men whom I had never seen before, some of them clearly marked by their dress as Eastern European Jews, crowded about, seeking to share our burden or at least to touch the bier on which the coffin rested. We finally halted opposite a tombstone bearing the name of Jacob Herzl, who had preceded his son to the grave by scarcely two years.

*   *   *

Dr. Siegmund Werner, Managing Editor of *Die Welt*, asked me soon after Herzl's death if I would help prepare the magazine's memorial issue, which was to appear on

July 8. I agreed with the reservation that I was in no state to write anything about the funeral, Herzl himself or the significance of his untimely loss. Instead, I gathered together, for publication in full or listing by name, the countless messages of condolence. At the head of those printed in *Die Welt* was a telegram received by the Zionist Action Committee from the King of Italy, followed by messages from the Grand Dukes of Baden and Hesse and from Austrian Prime Minister Ernst von Koerber. The long list of persons who had expressed sympathy included outstanding names in the Austrian Government, the Protestant clergy, and the world of art, journalism, the theater, commerce and industry. Nor were the messages couched in the usual stereotyped language; rather, they had an individual quality that gave them the ring of sincerity and, in the case of those from Zionist adherents, conveyed a sense of truly heart-felt grief.

From a sick-bed in Paris, Max Nordau wired Herzl's widow: "In such sorrow, there is no comfort; friends can do nothing but weep with you."

And to the Zionist Action Committee he sent the following telegram:

"Stunned by the terrible blow, I am struggling in vain for composure. Our loss is irreparable. Now that he has departed so incredibly long before his time, our unhappy people will first come to realize what it possessed in Herzl. I know that I am not exaggerating under the effect of recent sorrow when I lament that such a combination of love for the Jewish people, faith in its future, heroism, self-sacrifice, inexhaustible fertility of mind, strength of will, and patience had not been seen, and will not again be seen, for thousands of years. We shall weep for him eternally, but, in order that our sorrow may bear fruit, we must rouse ourselves to go on working in his spirit. For Herzl there can be but one worthy monument: his completed work."

47

FOLLOWING is a portion of Herzl's will, which he signed on May 23, 1900:

"5. My writings, with the exception of the Zionist diary, be brought out in a collected edition if a publisher can be found. My collected works should include all my *feuilletons*, lead articles, plays, etc.

"I should like Professor Kellner to handle the publication together with Erwin Rosenberger.

"6. If possible, I should also like to entrust these two gentlemen with the publication of my diary on the Zionist movement, which already totals seven volumes."

Not until some two months after Herzl's death did I learn of these provisions in his will. In September 1904, the above-mentioned Professor Kellner (whom the reader has already met briefly in an earlier chapter) and I received an invitation to speak to David Wolffsohn, an intimate friend of Herzl's whom the latter had named an executor of his will. After reading the relevant passages to us, Wolffsohn informed us that the executors had decided to publish Herzl's collected writings on Zionism and to entrust the work of preparation to us.

My part in this undertaking was to be twofold. First of all, since I had been an editor of *Die Welt* from the summer of 1897 to the summer of 1900, I was to prepare a list of Herzl's major contributions to the magazine during that period. In addition, Wolffsohn asked the two of us to look through Herzl's papers for possible material for the book. As it worked out, Professor Kellner inventoried the contents of one drawer and turned the remainder over to me.

Every day for several weeks, I went out to Herzl's home at No. 29 *Haizingergasse,* went through the papers stored in his desk, and listed what I found. Frau Herzl was invariably very helpful; she clarified the meaning of various items and, unless something of a personal nature was involved, opened sealed envelopes for me when their contents seemed worth investigating. If she was not always beaming as she watched the daily intruder rummage through her late husband's possessions, it was surely understandable.

When I finally finished my work, I had numbered 127 individual items or bundles of papers under various headings and had used an alphabetical listing for a few others. I placed in a separate drawer sixteen items which seemed to merit publication or at least a reference in the projected Zionist book.

During this period, I met Moriz Reichenfeld, a relative of Herzl's who was deputy director of the Vienna *Union-bank.* Reichenfeld, Wolffsohn and Herzl's friend Johann Kremenezky were the guardians of Herzl's children. They also acted as his literary trustees, and Professor Kellner and I received our instructions from them.

The book on which we were working was published in July 1905 by the Jewish Publishing House in Berlin as the *Zionist Writings of Theodor Herzl.* The royalties went to Herzl's family.

Some time after these events, I received a visit from Herr York-Steiner, a member of the committee which supervised publication of *Die Welt*. To my complete surprise, he offered me the managing editorship of the magazine. I replied that my medical career did not leave me sufficient time to cope with the work involved. Besides, I planned eventually to leave Vienna and take up the life of a ship's doctor. . . .

In December 1907, I at last realized my old ambition: I journeyed to Trieste and went to sea as a ship's doctor. It was many years before I returned to Vienna again.

48

THE MANY LETTERS and other papers which I have preserved from the Herzl days have had an adventurous career. Before I went to sea, I packed them in a small trunk and sent them to my sister Malvine Schick in Bohemia for safekeeping. During all the long years when I roamed the world as a ship's doctor—including the hectic period of the First World War—she guarded them faithfully.

When I finally settled in Vienna once again after my retirement, I had my sister send the trunk back to me. But my Herzl memorabilia and I were not fated to remain together for long. The Nazi annexation of Austria in 1938 forced me to flee Vienna, and among the property which I left behind with some Christian friends was the trunkful of papers.

When the bombs began falling on Vienna in the latter part of World War II, I virtually gave up hope of seeing the Herzl papers again. But then, not long after V-E Day, I received a letter in Florence, where my wife and I had found refuge: My Viennese friends wrote to say that they had been bombed out; their house had been completely wrecked . . . except for the storeroom containing my trunk and other possessions! It was almost as if the deadly projectile had shown human forbearance when it missed by barely three feet the momentos of my years with Theodor Herzl.

*   *   *

Now I hope the reader will forgive me if I mention two purely personal matters for the sake of the record:

(1) The index to Herzl's *Diaries,* which were brought out by the former Jewish Publishing House of Berlin, lists me as "Rosenberger, F." The compiler of the index obviously confused me with my brother Felix, a Viennese physician.

(2) My listing in the index to Dr. Alex Bein's biography of Herzl (published in 1934) refers the reader to page 336. The latter page, however, contains no mention of me; it refers, instead, to Adam Rosenberg, a New York attorney who helped draw up the Zionist movement's Program at the First Zionist Congress in Basle. I have no wish to filch any credit which rightfully belongs to Mr. Rosenberg. During the First Zionist Congress, as it happens, I was not in Basle but in *Die Welt's* editorial offices in Vienna.

49

IN THE SUMMER OF 1951, my wife and I visited Vienna to spend a few weeks with my brother and sister. Inevitably, during this short stay, I found myself seeking out the various places that recalled the days when I knew Theodor Herzl.

I turned my steps first toward the house at No. 6 *Berggasse*, where Herzl had once lived. It was there that he had invited me to join the staff of *Die Welt* and there, in his study, that we had worked together to advance his ideal of a Jewish state. The building had suffered relatively little war damage; all five stories were intact and occupied. Only on one side had the plaster largely fallen off, exposing the brick, and the double window in the corner from which Herzl had sometimes gazed down into the street during a pause in his work was still stopped up with paper to replace the missing glass.

It was curious how different the big corner house seemed from the picture of it that I had stored in my memory. What I saw as I stood there now was a quite ordinary, rather drab-looking apartment building. Was it the ravages of time and war that had wrought the change? Or was it rather that in those earlier days it had been transfigured for me by the fact that it was Theodor Herzl's home?

I entered the house through the big outer door that I knew so well, passed through the smaller doorway inside, and walked across the entrance-hall to the staircase on the left. Everything was just the same: the wide stone steps, the iron banister, the three landings to each story. When

I reached the second floor, I turned to the right, approached the familiar door . . . and caught myself just as I was about to ring.

As I was leaving the house, I met the *concierge*, a young woman of perhaps thirty. I asked her if she had ever heard of a Dr. Herzl who had once lived there. "Dr. Herzl?" she said. "When was that?" When she heard the year 1897, she threw up her hands in astonishment: "That was long before I came into the world.". . .

The next stop in my memory-crowded itinerary was No. 9 *Türkenstrasse*, which had once housed *Die Welt's* editorial offices. The four-story building, where Herzl had made his daily afternoon visits, looked down at me seemingly unchanged. So did the house at No. 11 *Rembrandtstrasse*, a quarter- hour distant by foot. There at the headquarters of the "Zion" Society—later to serve as the first, temporary editorial offices of *Die Welt*—I had risen to utter a few words one evening in Herzl's presence and thereby opened an unforgettable chapter in my life.

The Jägerhof Café, once a favorite meeting place of Vienna's Jewish students, had vanished from the face of the earth. Its place at No. 22 *Porzellangasse* was occupied by a motion-picture equipment warehouse. Next I searched for the Café Central, where I had once spent so many hours combing the daily papers for suitable items for *Die Welt*. The building at No. 14 *Herrengasse* was still standing, but the café was nowhere to be seen; in its place was a business firm.

Another Viennese coffee-house which had contributed its mite to the ultimate founding of a Jewish state had emerged from the war not only intact but thoroughly renovated and embellished. This was the establishment at No. 14 *Döblinger Haupt-Strasse* where Herzl and I had sat one summer day in 1897, distilling *Die Welt's* special issue on the First Zionist Congress from a huge sheaf of papers which Herzl had brought back from Basle that very morning. Across the street, a large sign, "Printer and Publisher," testified that the print-shop we had used that summer was still in business after more than half a century.

Not far from this spot had been the garden restaurant where Herzl and I had often had lunch after a morning spent in reading proofs and making up pages at the printer's. Unhappily, the fondly remembered bit of greenery had been engulfed by the great city; in its place was a tall building whose ground floor was occupied by a druggist.

At last, I completed my journey into the past by boarding the trolley and traveling across town to the corner of *Schleifmühlgasse* and *Rechte Wienzeile*. I was looking for the building of the *Wiener Mode* magazine, in whose print-shop the first issues of *Die Welt* had seen the light of day. It was here that I had entered a composing room for the first time and that Herzl had patiently initiated me into the mysteries of printing and proofreading. When I arrived at my destination, there was no sign of the *Wiener Mode;* the building which I remembered its having tenanted had been transformed into the "Three Crowns Hotel." Wondering if I might possibly have made an error, I entered the hotel and addressed myself to an elderly man who appeared to be the manager. "Yes," he said, "the *Wiener Mode* was here at one time—but that was many years ago."

50

THEODOR HERZL IS THE FATHER of the modern Zionist movement. In our day, he was the first to declare boldly and openly that a Jewish state was both necessary and possible. Others had proposed establishing Jewish colonies on the territory and under the sovereignty of another state. Herzl was the first to call for an independent, sovereign, internationally recognized Jewish commonwealth on its own territory—a national state like any other in the world.

It took tremendous courage for Herzl to launch his new movement. Few of us today realize how utopian, absurd and, indeed, utterly insane the very concept of a Jewish state seemed to most people when Herzl first published his historic little book in 1896. It was only through his tireless efforts that the skeptics were gradually disarmed and were brought to the realization that what had seemed a chimera was actually a practical, attainable goal.

Nor was Herzl content merely to bring his idea into the world and win public respect for it; he did everything in his power to transform it into reality. He created a variety of instruments for that purpose: the Zionist congresses, the weekly magazine *Die Welt,* the Jewish Colonial Trust, and the worldwide Zionist organization. And the source from which all these institutions drew their inspiration and strength was Herzl himself.

Theodor Herzl united in his personality all the qualities required for his mission as founder of a Jewish state. The indefinable power of attraction that radiated from him made the Jewish masses rally to him and give him their allegiance. The authority that flashed from his eyes and spoke from his lips enabled him to guide his followers, once they were won, along the path he marked out. And the force of his intellect, including his gift of eloquence, engraved his concept of a Jewish state so deeply in the minds of others that it remained alive in the decades that followed his death and ultimately bore fruit in the creation of the State of Israel.

No one could have been more ideally suited than Herzl to plead the cause of Zionism before influential non-Jewish figures—before statesmen, princes, kings and emperors. And, indeed, he made so persuasive a spokesman of his people, that, as we have already seen, he was offered a tract of British territory in East Africa on which to establish an autonomus Jewish community—a plan which, though it came to nought, helped to impress the world with the feasibility of the Jewish-state idea.

Every idea, however, lofty it may be and however imperious the necessity that impels it, must nevertheless find an individual who can embody it and carry it to victory. Theodor Herzl seemed predestined for his task. He possessed extraordinary energy, unflagging perseverance, humility in the face of failure, and a capacity to identify himself with his work to the point of sacrificing his most vital personal interests.

The effects of Herzl's life and work are still felt in our day; the call that he sounded still echoes. Of all the legacies he left, perhaps the most precious was his example.

*   *   *

The letters from Herzl quoted in this book and published here for the first time, as well as the other documents referred to, are now in the Herzl Archives which are preserved in the Zionist Central Archives in Jerusalem.